Raising the Tech Bar at Your Library

RAISING THE TECH BAR AT YOUR LIBRARY

Improving Services to Meet User Needs

Nick D. Taylor

LIBRARIES UNLIMITED™

An Imprint of ABC-CLIO, LLC

Santa Barbara, California • Denver, Colorado

Library of Congress Cataloging-in-Publication Data

Names: Taylor, Nick D., author.
Title: Raising the tech bar at your library : improving services to meet user
    needs / Nick D. Taylor.
Description: Santa Barbara, California : Libraries Unlimited, an imprint of
    ABC-CLIO, LLC, [2017] | Includes bibliographical references and index.
Identifiers: LCCN 2017018675 (print) | LCCN 2017000171 (ebook) | ISBN
    9781440844973 (ebook) | ISBN 9781440844966 (paperback : acid-free paper)
Subjects: LCSH: Public libraries—Information technology. | Libraries and the
    Internet. | Public services (Libraries) | Technological literacy—Study and teaching. |
    Librarians—Effect of technological innovations on. | Library users—Effect of technological
    innovations on. | Public libraries—United States—Case studies.
Classification: LCC Z678.9 (print) | LCC Z678.9 .T39 2017 (ebook) | DDC
    020.285/4678—dc23
LC record available at https://lccn.loc.gov/2017018675

ISBN: 978-1-4408-4496-6
EISBN: 978-1-4408-4497-3

21 20 19 18 17   1 2 3 4 5

This book is also available as an eBook.

Libraries Unlimited
An Imprint of ABC-CLIO, LLC

ABC-CLIO, LLC
130 Cremona Drive, P.O. Box 1911
Santa Barbara, California 93116-1911
www.abc-clio.com

This book is printed on acid-free paper ∞
Manufactured in the United States of America

To Tracy and Fiction Beer Company for making the brainstorming sessions highly enjoyable.

To Corvus Coffee Roasters for the caffeine, Wi-Fi, and seating space!

Contents

1

Why Raise the Bar?

INTRODUCTION

Raising the bar for tech services in libraries means going above and beyond basic technology offerings. Basic offerings are what you're likely to find in nearly 90 percent of libraries: computer classes, public computers, e-books, and Wi-Fi (Clark & Perry, 2015). To further improve public perception of libraries and to advocate for even more meaningful usage of these community institutions, the purpose of this book is to encourage libraries to focus on ways to improve their existing tech services or even to expand their offerings. For example, your library may provide computer classes, but what can you do to make sure the ideas are sticking, that your students are truly learning? You may have grand plans to purchase a 3D printer, but how will you ensure the community wants it, and then how will you convince your superiors it's a great idea?

Questions like these inspired this book. Hopefully it will equip you with the tools needed to do what's mentioned above and more. Consider it guidance for the average library and librarian, for those who are looking to expand upon and improve their technology services. It is a practical guide, but is also intended to inspire.

This first chapter presents the groundwork for the rest of the book. It provides a basic framework of how libraries came to be tech hubs and why advancing tech services in libraries is so important. Chapters 2 through 6 feature more specific subjects like staffing, physical space, and learning. The final chapter reflects on current trends and the future so you can continue to anticipate ways to iterate and improve your tech services.

The author and the colleagues he has consulted while creating this book work for tech departments in libraries that have raised the bar when it comes to tech services. Makerspaces, coding initiatives, unique computer classes, and other complex tech interactions have become the norm in these libraries. As a result, the author draws on his own experiences and those of his colleagues to help inform his opinions. The libraries used for inspiration, Arapahoe Libraries and Denver Public Library, are medium- to large-sized library systems in the metropolitan area of Denver, both of which have implemented sweeping technology services in the form of initiatives, staffing, and programming. But this isn't a local phenomenon; libraries all over the country, and indeed all over the world, are doing innovative things with technology.

First and foremost, advice in this book takes into consideration that iterating and improving upon your technology services should not necessarily have a lot of dollar signs attached. More important is library philosophy, or attitude. The author acknowledges that there are libraries of all sizes and budgets, from single-employee rural libraries to modern, urban, trendsetting libraries, and one size certainly does not fit all. Arapahoe Libraries and Denver Public Library are on the whole more willing to take risks, especially when it comes to budgeting. Although well-allocated money can be a fast track to improving your tech offerings, libraries of all sizes and budgets share a passion for great technology services. With this in mind, the author offers suitable alternatives and mentions where there's room for savings whenever possible. (Consult the "Affordable Alternatives" sections at the end of chapters 1–6 for suggestions.)

SHORT HISTORY OF TECH IN LIBRARIES

To understand why tech services in libraries are important and why you should be passionate about improving on them even further, a short history of tech in libraries is in order. Once you see how libraries have evolved into tech-forward spaces full of tablets, 3D printers, and makerspaces, you will have a much better idea of how you and your library can move forward.

By far the most influential technological innovation for libraries in recent memory is the Internet. Libraries were one of the first public institutions to fully harness it. Long before Internet access was as ubiquitous as it is today, libraries offered public computers with access to this burgeoning technology. Though Internet access had been adopted and used in libraries earlier, expansion truly began in the mid- to late 1990s. In the short span between 1994 and 2002, the percentage of public libraries connected to the Internet grew from 21 to nearly 100 percent (Bertot, Jaeger, Wahl, & Sigler, 2011). These numbers show that libraries quickly recognized the need for Internet access and rapidly adapted to offer the service to their users.

As a result, libraries began to add more computers for public access and computer labs. Information retrieval in libraries was more important than ever, but now the tools were increasingly in the hands of the patrons rather than only accessible through a librarian at a reference desk. This change in the way the average person accessed information ushered in the information age, the era in which Internet access has become common and ubiquitous, when information seekers turn to the Internet and digitized information for their needs more frequently than to physical media such as encyclopedias and periodicals. Herrera-Viedma and Lopez-Gijon (2013) observed that libraries and librarians have in some ways been replaced by, respectively, the Internet and Google. They are not the only ones to think this. In fact, many people, including some politicians and public officials, hold the mistaken view that there is no need for libraries now that we have the Internet. The Internet serves as the repository of information that the traditional library was; the search engine retrieves said information. Since physical media used to be the average library's primary focus, this has signified a significant shift. Herrera-Viedma and Lopez-Gijon's suggestion is for the library to forget about being an information repository and instead work toward building great relationships with library users through providing an educational community institution, a community gathering place for a meeting of the minds. Library philosophy has remained the same in the information age; libraries continue to provide access to resources and information, just through different media. This information cannot be held in your hands the way a reference book or printed government document could be, but libraries provide just as much (if not more) meaningful information and context today as they have in the past. Yet despite the similarities in what the end user ultimately receives, the information age has changed the roles of modern-day librarians and the needs that their communities prioritize.

For example, in the information age it is less common for public librarians to field basic reference questions from their patrons. The answer to a question such as "What's the date of Arbor Day in 2018?" could now easily be found by most people with access to the Internet and a search engine. Reference work is still a primary focus in academic environments and is still an important service, but it cannot be denied that Internet access has changed what patrons ask of librarians and what they need, especially from their local public libraries.

Overall, Internet access was the single most influential factor in the shift from the libraries of old, the brick-and-mortar buildings full of physical media and information, to the libraries of now, harbingers of electronic information gathering and nontraditional educational opportunities. It is the single flash point that sparked a need for increasingly complex technology services in libraries.

WHAT'S HAPPENING IN LIBRARIES NOW?

In the ongoing discussion about Internet access and usage in the United States, former President Barack Obama and the United Nations have stated that the Internet is no longer just a resource; it is a basic utility not only to thrive, but to live (Kravets, 2011; Olanoff, 2015). Despite this societal change, as many as one in four Americans do not have Internet at home, according to the U.S. Census Bureau (File & Ryan, 2014). In an increasingly connected society in which the Internet provides access to important amenities such as banking, medical information, and e-government sources, this is a huge issue for many people.

As a result, Internet usage and computer access have become a signifying feature of the modern library experience. Instead of utilizing their local public libraries to find information or to check out physical media, library patrons are visiting the library for Wi-Fi access. According to the 2014 Digital Inclusion Survey, there was a 9 percent increase in the number of libraries that provide free wireless Internet access between 2012 and 2014, bringing the percentage to 98 percent of all libraries (Clark & Perry, 2015). A 2016 Pew report stated that "29% of library-using Americans 16 and older said they had gone to libraries to use computers, the internet, or a public Wi-Fi network. (That amounts to 23% of all Americans ages 16 and above.)" (Horrigan, 2016). The rapid increase in Wi-Fi adoption in libraries and the fact that nearly all public libraries see the need to offer it further illustrate just how necessary this amenity is to libraries and communities.

Hand in hand with the increased desire for Wi-Fi is the use of personal devices in many public libraries. A 2015 Pew study reported that "64% of Americans own a smartphone, up from 5% in early 2014" (Smith, 2015). Rather than using the public access computers, some patrons bring in personal devices to connect to the library's Internet. Since personal, Internet-enabled devices such as smartphones have become more affordable and more of a necessity for the average consumer, it only makes sense that they would connect them to their local library's wireless Internet.

Since 2014, with 42 percent of American adults owning a tablet computer (Mobile Technology Fact Sheet, 2013) and smartphones becoming even more common, digital content to download and access on these devices has become an increasingly desired service in libraries. Even earlier, a 2012 survey conducted by the American Library Association (ALA) reported a 9.1 percent increase in libraries offering access to e-books over the course of a year, bringing the total to 76.3 percent of all libraries (American Library Association, 2014). Third-party e-content providers such as Overdrive,

Hoopla, and Zinio have become common in many libraries as this service has become more sought after.

Considering the way e-content providers evolved, it is not surprising how popular e-content has become for libraries and their patrons. At first, Overdrive offered most e-books in EPUB, a format that was not fully compatible with Amazon's highly popular Kindle. Overdrive also offered most audiobooks in WMA format, another less user-friendly format to use on the leading portable music player, Apple's iPod. As you can imagine, there was demand from libraries and their patrons for Overdrive to offer more user-friendly formats, such as Kindle Book format for the Kindle and mp3 files for the iPod. Today, perhaps because libraries and their patrons' preferences were made clear, both formats are available through Overdrive (Sockel, 2014). The fact that consumer demand was enough to convince Overdrive and Amazon to work to solve this issue is a good example of just how popular these services have become and how much library patrons' needs have changed, skewing in the direction of technology-related services.

The increase in Wi-Fi availability, pervasiveness of personal Internet-enabled devices, and rising circulation of e-materials demonstrate the marked difference in the needs of patrons compared to just 10 years ago. These findings imply that patrons who do visit the library are there not only for physical materials or reference assistance, but also for technological amenities such as Wi-Fi. Moreover, the ability to access e-resources from anywhere means that library patrons can check out materials in the comfort of their homes, away from the brick-and-mortar library building. Patrons also use their own devices with library Wi-Fi and ask for reference assistance more sparingly. These changes all largely point to independent library usage: patrons who value the space and amenities of the library rather than reference help from their friendly neighborhood librarian. One library had reason to believe these trends were affecting its services; a study found an increase in Web page views and decrease in overall reference questions, resulting in the elimination of its reference desk in favor of more generalized in-person help and online assistance (Meldrem, Mardis, & Johnson, 2005). These factors combined indicate that brick-and-mortar library buildings and traditional reference assistance are becoming less of a priority to library patrons.

So with all of these trends, why aren't more people concerned about the end of libraries? And why do librarians balk at the latest article or debate about their obsolescence? Let's look at why we are excited about this shift and how libraries can be more relevant and important than ever.

WHY THIS IS IMPORTANT: THE DIGITAL DIVIDE

The changing priorities of library patrons and the decreasing need to use library services in a traditional way should be a call to arms for libraries.

They need to change their offerings to maintain relevance in today's society. Many librarians are frustrated by the misconception that libraries are dusty old warehouses full of books, staffed by bespectacled elderly women with buns in their hair. One of the best ways to combat this image is to introduce new and innovative ways to provide service to library communities. Although basic tech services such as computer classes and public Internet access have been much appreciated and utilized by past and current generations, libraries need to keep pushing to become even more tech literate if they are going to remain relevant to future generations. The ubiquity with which libraries offer these basic tech services means that the philosophy is already there; libraries recognize that these services are core to library patrons. Now they just need to work toward evolution and improvement.

One reason that tech services are core to libraries is that they provide access and education to people from all walks of life. Libraries act as equalizers. This philosophy can best be understood in the context of the *digital divide*, defined as the separation between various demographics and their access to technology. This divide can be due to geographic location, socioeconomic status, and/or a variety of other largely external factors (Public Libraries & the Internet, n.d.). For example, some mountain communities in Colorado rely on their local libraries for Internet access, not because the average household cannot afford it, but because their Internet service providers (ISPs) do not have coverage in their remote area. The same is true in many rural settings and other places facing geographic challenges. Just by virtue of having publicly available Internet and computers, libraries have been integral in closing the digital divide in many communities. In a 2015 Pew survey, folks were asked why they do not use the Internet. For many the answer was relevance, not seeing the importance or need. For just about the same number, 32 percent of respondents, the issue was usability, meaning the user would need guidance or assistance in accessing the Internet. Another 7 percent cited the issue of availability (Rainie, 2015). Availability and assistance are exactly what libraries can provide when it comes to Internet access!

The digital divide has been an especially pressing concern in the past decade due to the increasing pressure to be technologically literate in today's society. Finding the best deal online for a new appliance, keeping in touch with family and friends through social media, and even finding jobs are becoming crucial, not optional, skills. Supporting this trend, the ALA's Public Library Funding and Technology Access Study 2011–2012 (2012) reported a 36 percent increase in computer class attendance at libraries. This correlates with the desire of more people to educate themselves and to gain basic computer skills. It also shows that as time goes by, these skills are more sought out. Whereas in the 1990s and early 2000s computer classes were usually taken by those looking to improve their résumés or learn a new job skill, these newer statistics suggest that computer skills are now essential for a larger chunk of the population.

Since lack of these skills and limited Internet access put individuals at such a disadvantage, these are the most important issues current and future libraries can tackle. Internet access is an especially glaring problem. Current statistics show that having a device with some sort of Internet access is fairly common, but that device may not necessarily be a computer. Some 19 percent of American adults are smartphone dependent, meaning there is no other means of Internet access available to them. As one might assume, this is most often due to financial restrictions. Paying a subscription for home Internet access in addition to a phone plan and other monthly bills is too great a cost for individuals of lower socioeconomic status (Rainie, 2015). Clearly those with lower earning power consider Internet access a necessity, so they find the most affordable avenue through which to get it. This trend can be partially attributed to the fact that ISPs in America face little to no competition in most geographic areas, providing no incentive for them to lower prices (Brodkin, 2015). As a result, having Internet access at home can be more onerous and expensive than using a phone and data plan alone. The current state of Internet access has forced many Americans to seek out alternatives, libraries' open and free Internet being a saving grace for many.

Adding to the severity of the issue, 40 percent or more of smartphone owners use them to access medical information, banking, and job applications (Smith, 2015). The tasks involved in using these services can be incredibly challenging to accomplish on a smartphone touch keyboard with the limited data allowances that phone companies enforce. In addition, many important governmental services are increasingly available through online means only, whether forms must be printed from online or filled out online. A study on e-government resources in libraries found that over 96 percent of American libraries have provided some sort of assistance in utilizing e-governmental resources, such as applying for unemployment, applying for citizenship, or finding tax forms (American Library Association, 2014). Since so many libraries provide these services, it seems likely that many people come to the library because the information they need or task they need to perform is most easily accomplished or only accomplished through online means. It seems that e-government services would be nearly impossible to access for some members of the public without the free Internet and computer access that libraries provide.

Many if not most libraries both passively and actively provide resources that close the digital divide, so talking about the importance of libraries in battling the digital divide is redundant for many. Everybody knows that Internet access in libraries is a core service. But reminding ourselves how and why libraries have become the sole provider for free Internet for many gives us perspective on why and how they can push technological services even further.

WHY THIS IS IMPORTANT: MAKERSPACES AND STEM

In the interest of providing ever-improving technology access and service, libraries have expanded upon the digital divide philosophy beyond Internet and computer access. One example of this expansion is the makerspaces and media labs that have appeared in public libraries. One of the first of these spaces created was the Fab Lab in Fayetteville, New York, Free Library, which boasts tools such as 3D printers, sewing machines, a CNC mill, and a button maker. Lauren Britton (2012), an employee at the Fab Lab, stated that Internet access and computers alone do not close the digital divide; there are other tools and strategies to provide access and education to the community. These spaces supply tools that are inherently valuable to library patrons because they are too expensive for one user or household to purchase. In the same way that free Internet provides access for a user who cannot afford it at home, a fabrication tool or a sewing machine can also act as an equalizer.

As Internet access and computers become more necessary home utilities rather than luxury perks, libraries have used makerspaces to provide access to technology and tools that are less likely to be found in their communities' homes. Whereas a digital divide–related issue in lower socioeconomic status communities is Internet and computer access, libraries in more affluent areas can do their part through makerspaces. A community member may have a smartphone with which to film a video, but not the software to edit the finished product. An aspiring musician may have written songs and have the skills to perform them, but no quiet, soundproofed space in which to record. Libraries can help. This represents libraries' persistence in closing the digital divide on a macroscale, attracting larger audiences of individuals who lack access to these tools and devices. And there's no saying that libraries cannot still be everything to everyone: they are able to provide Internet and computer access to those in need while still finding ways to attract new audiences and demographics with amenities like makerspaces. Of course, library patrons of a lower socioeconomic status would also benefit from makerspaces, but libraries in those areas often lack the funding to fully realize them, or need to spend their capital on meeting the basic needs of those patrons first.

The creation of these makerspaces and hackerspaces has shifted programming philosophies at some libraries to encompass STEM (science, technology, engineering, math) related programming. (It should be noted that this acronym sometimes appears as STEAM to incorporate art as well. Keep this in mind for any potential craft spaces your library might consider!) STEM education has become a priority for many schools because of growing industries like Web design demand coding, engineering, and science. The Equation for Change predicts that the next decade will see a 17 percent growth in STEM jobs, while non-STEM jobs will grow 12 percent ("Solving the Diversity Dilemma," 2015). As a result, many educators and libraries have taken it upon themselves to encourage STEM programming and education in their respective fields.

Libraries, especially those equipped with makerspaces or media labs, are perfectly poised to help teach STEM skills. Coding clubs, Web design workshops, and circuitry programs for children and teens have become more common in libraries. For example, the Denver Public Library hosted its first DevCamp in summer 2014, a weeklong camp that utilized Web developers and library employees to teach teens HTML, CSS, and JavaScript. The forethought and success of the program garnered the library an award from the Urban Libraries Council as top innovator of 2015 (Chuang, 2015). The fantastic built-from-scratch Web sites that came out of the camp would have been reward enough, but the national attention and recognition they received truly shows how adopting tech-forward teaching philosophies can be a net positive for libraries.

STEM programs give libraries a reason to work hard toward tech-centric initiatives, because we know we are working to ensure the future of both libraries and the people we are teaching. Although public schools are carrying the torch with a number of STEM initiatives of their own, they cannot be the lone source. Learning does not happen only in schools; libraries can also provide great opportunities for learning, usually on an informal basis.

That informal learning also means that libraries could have a huge impact on industries that lack a diverse workforce, such as Web development. A study showed that informal learning environments benefit minority women in STEM fields. The idea is that such learning can help unify STEM concepts with the background or knowledge women already possess (Hopwood, 2012). Libraries, the great equalizers, can provide the right environment for STEM tools and education to demographics that are not often encouraged to pursue these fields. Over time, this can lead science- and math-heavy industries toward more equal gender ratios and demographics. These small interactions in public libraries can potentially spark a lifelong passion that leads to a career path that may never have been considered achievable without the access libraries can provide.

Similarly, researchers at the Massachusetts Institute of Technology have shown that informal learning in public spaces like libraries can also be the key to maximum engagement for youth. HOMAGO, which stands for hang out, mess around, and geek out, is a philosophy for exposing youth to educational content. The three are meant to be stages of learning: hanging out being socially based, messing around as experimentation, and geeking out as truly delving into the content and becoming an expert (Columbus Museum of Art, 2014). Utilizing this simple philosophy, it is possible for libraries to engage youth with STEM activities and makerspaces to help guide them toward productive but fun activities that can lead to new hobbies or even future careers.

Since there is a national push for STEM education and there are so many organizations dedicated to it, now is a great time to apply for grant opportunities and memberships. Organizations from NASA to IMLS (Institution of Museum and Library Services) have a number of STEM-related grants that can help launch makerspaces, STEM programming, hardware—whatever you need to get started. Whether the service is a Web developer teaching teens to make a Web site or a simple LEGO program for children, infusing library services and programming with STEM is entirely achievable.

HOW TO CONVINCE YOUR COMMUNITY AND THE PEOPLE IN CHARGE

Hopefully by now you are equipped with some knowledge to help you convince your community and superiors to reevaluate and improve upon tech services in your library. The numbers are on your side. More likely than not, your community is full of users with personal devices and an interest in accessing free Wi-Fi. Those users have laid the groundwork for expanded, more innovative tech services at the library. If they have already found that Internet access and e-resources are great amenities, offering more complex computer classes, opening a makerspace, or hosting coding events is not much of a stretch. Making these things happen with limited staff and financial resources may seem like an uphill battle, but rest assured that advice and solutions for these issues are available in later chapters of this book.

Any community and its library would likely benefit from expanded tech services, but don't rush in without careful consideration. Be cognizant of your community and its demographics. Although the numbers and statistics cited here speak to the majority of communities, you know your own community best. If you have a local music school, a media lab equipped with microphones may be your best investment. If you have a cadre of knitters who regularly meet at the library already, consider a craft-themed makerspace. Asking your patrons what they want can never hurt, and it all but guarantees a captive audience with plenty of buy-in once you open the space.

These compelling arguments will hopefully convince you and your superiors that improving upon your existing tech services is crucial to your library's continued relevance. The ideas and tools here fall in line well with library service philosophy and have garnered attention and accord for a number of early adopter libraries, so there is little to lose. If some of these ideas are accomplishable on a small scale, give them a try, document your successes, and take those to your superiors. Tangible evidence of results like pictures, statistics, and stories of success will speak on a greater level than our words or your own.

AFFORDABLE ALTERNATIVES

E-books and Wi-Fi are two of the harbingers of new tech services and innovation in libraries today. Both can be expensive in terms of implementation and upkeep. Unfortunately, many ISPs either do not offer an educational discount or do not consider libraries educational institutions and thus do not offer them a discount. Fortunately there are a few services to keep in mind for cheap or free Internet. FreedomPop is an ISP that is trying to buck the trend of monopolized or overly expensive mobile and Internet service. If you are in its service area, this could be an option. Municipal wireless Internet is also becoming more and more common, so perhaps your library can be an advocate for your city or community to explore that possibility (see more about municipal wireless Internet in chapter 7). You may also consider allocating more of your budget to support Internet access in your library building, using our arguments and data to support your requests.

E-books pose a challenge when it comes to finances as well. Many e-book providers have to deal with regulations and limitations imposed by book publishers, such as having "metered access," which means an e-book from one publisher can only circulate a certain number of times before it expires and then a new title must be purchased. Similar to the ISP problem, Overdrive is overwhelmingly the e-content provider to 90 percent of U.S. public libraries (Seave, 2013). Some libraries have fought back against this monopoly, most recently the State Library of New South Wales. The New South Wales library put together an e-book collection of Australian authors and other local content, effectively building its own platform that circumvents third-party providers like Overdrive by negotiating directly with publishers, authors, and other content providers (LaRue, 2016). Libraries interested in participating in the movement to circumvent the demands of big publishers or seeking a sympathetic ear can visit IndyReads at indyreads.odlio.us. A less revolutionary option but nevertheless worth mentioning is Project Gutenberg, which provides thousands of free, largely public domain, e-book titles. Project Gutenberg is a fantastic back pocket tool for any library or librarian looking to offer digital content affordably.

2

Gauging Your Community's Needs

- Needs Assessment
- Pitfalls of Data Collection
- Data Collection Best Practices
- Creating a Tech Plan
- What Problem Can We Solve?
- Aligning with Your Strategic Plan
- Affordable Alternatives

Now that you've learned why tech in libraries is important, the next consideration in the process of improving tech services is discovering what exactly your community needs. Communities vary in size, affluence, and many other ways, so tech services' needs will similarly vary by geographic location. Assuming that every library computer lab needs, say, a large number of public computers, is a mistake. Perhaps the library is in an affluent area where its patrons mostly have personal laptops, or the community is very small and only needs a handful of public computers. These are the types of issues that should be considered in any and all decisions made while improving tech services.

NEEDS ASSESSMENT

The most common tool for evaluating demographics and finding areas to improve is a community needs assessment. This is pretty much what it sounds like: a survey that determines the needs of the local community and how they compare to what an institution currently offers. The assessment typically includes a study of local demographics, a survey, an interview, or any other combination of information-gathering techniques. A community needs assessment can be done on a small scale, such as a paper survey for patrons inside the library, or on a large scale, hiring an external firm and forming focus groups. In any case, your first step is data collection.

PITFALLS OF DATA COLLECTION

A common data collection tactic for libraries is the survey, usually conducted inside the library or linked from the library's Web site. While this can be effective when used in tandem with other means of data collection, the survey can also be a problematic way to collect data due to a heavy reliance on anecdotal evidence. The survey can also produce tunnel vision, as your data may only be coming from inside your library, or from those who access the library's Web site, but will be used to determine an entire community's needs. To put it another way, if you were to conduct a survey inside your library or on your Web site to ask how to improve your tech services, you would immediately filter your survey participants down to those who already use the library and even further to those users who are willing to take time to do the survey. This could drastically restrict your audience and skew the meaningfulness of the data you collect. Users inside the library or on the Web site are more likely to be satisfied with its offerings and familiar with current services. On top of that, surveying only those people willing to stop what they are doing and provide feedback can bias your results by gathering information from the most vocal users, not necessarily your potential unheard demographics. Attracting new users to the library and making the library a better resource for the entire community means that you want data from outside your walls, collected in various ways.

In addition to the problematic nature of the sample pool, surveys limit the depth and breadth of responses community members are able to offer. The main problem with surveys is that they offer a limited scope of possible responses, since they always involve a list of answers (Williment, 2013). Bias is nearly impossible to avoid in a survey because the questions themselves strongly indicate the types of answers the survey givers are looking for. So in addition to the biased audience of library users, surveys won't get you data about your blind spots. They are likely to act as an echo chamber, which will make it difficult to effect any real change or offer new, useful services that might not have otherwise occurred to you.

Evaluative survey data can be augmented with demographic information about factors such as age, gender, wealth, and race. There are some tech-specific resources that can be useful in collecting relevant data. Lib2Gov (n.d.), an e-government source for libraries, suggests utilizing tools like the National Broadband map to educate yourself on broadband Internet availability in your area. The University of Maryland built and maintains the Digital Inclusion Survey Interactive Map, a handy tool that allows you to select your library to see data on Wi-Fi speed and types of tech offerings, mixed in with basic demographic data from the U.S. Census (Digital

Inclusion Survey, 2015). Since Internet access and availability are such important amenities in libraries today, these are fantastic tools to have in your back pocket.

Though these data are valuable, a cautionary note is in order. Do not read too heavily into demographic data like this, even data that pertain to a specialty like the Digital Inclusion Survey Interactive Map, because they tend to exclude a large portion of the community (Williment, 2013). Basic demographics provide only surface-level data that may not necessarily pertain to library use or anything of value. You might find data that show your area has a significant number of French speakers, but never see them in the library. Demographic data are helpful in tandem with other data, but frustratingly lack detail and specificity (Williment, 2013). This seems a sensible concern, since it can be a little too easy to make blanket assumptions based on demographic data. As any statistician will tell you, correlation does not imply causation (Goldin, 2015). This is not to say that demographic data cannot be helpful in decision making, only that they need to be just one part of a number of considerations regarding your community and never the only tool you use in your decision-making process.

DATA COLLECTION BEST PRACTICES

A good needs analysis of your community should utilize demographic data but not exclusively. A survey, especially one only conducted within the library's walls, will not yield the best results either. A recommended method is to integrate the community into the data gathering. By collaborating with the community outside the library, you are likely to obtain less biased results and will demonstrate a stronger commitment to facilitate meaningful change, certainly more so than just having an unstaffed table with paper or electronic surveys in the library.

Pursue these out-of-library sessions through partnerships, door-to-door canvassing, and community events (Williment, 2013). By communicating with those in your community who are not already regular library users, you will be able to gather valuable data from those who have not visited the library in a while. You'll also forge community connections unrelated to your data gathering that could blossom into productive partnerships on other fronts, such as programming or volunteer assistance.

In addition to being the most meaningful way to truly gauge your community's opinions about the library, out-of-library needs analysis just happens to be one of the more affordable data collection tactics. Volunteers are preferred data collectors, as they are less likely to have bias toward positive results than library employees. Although there are certainly firms and professionals that can be hired to collect data, tweak questions, and help you through this process, a small task force that gathers a large enough sample for your community can be just as effective. If your library has never used this tactic, even a small effort just to get started is an improvement over nothing or solely relying on in-library data collection.

However you choose to gather your data, it is important to ask questions about the library's technology offerings and what members of your community have available to them at home or elsewhere in the area. You might ask questions like the following:

- Do you own a personal computer?
- Does your home have Wi-Fi or other Internet access?
- Have you used the library for technology help? If not, would you like to?
- Have you paid for technology help in the past year? Where?
- Have you taken a computer class at the library? What topics would you like to learn?

Keep in mind that while you will have demographic information that can help guide your questions, hearing what people want straight from the source is also helpful. If an individual has not visited the library in some time, offer information about what is currently available at the library and probe to see what amenities, tech or otherwise, might attract that person back.

There are two factors to keep in mind while conducting an out-of-library needs analysis. One is that nearly one-third of library users are not aware of the full extent of what libraries have to offer (Rainie, 2014). As a result, the needs analysis done during your outreach effort will involve lots of informing and educating in addition to probing for data. This is totally acceptable and can secondarily serve the library as word-of-mouth outreach and promotion, but do be aware of this. Second, keep in mind that the public opinion of libraries is high: 90 percent of people surveyed said the library's closing would have an impact on their community (Rainie, 2014). This goes hand in hand with the public being uninformed about library offerings: people often have a relatively vague but largely positive opinion of the library. Consequently, you may have to work harder to get constructive criticism or a wish list of tech-related offerings from them.

CREATING A TECH PLAN

Once you have collected enough data from your community needs analysis, it's time to begin the process of creating a tech plan. A tech plan helps outline the process of taking the data from your community needs' analysis and turning them into tangible results, whether they are hardware, software, staff, or other tech amenities. Keep in mind that this plan encompasses a broad swath of your services, from your integrated library system to your Internet speed to your patron-facing technology services. It will provide the groundwork for future steps you can take based on the specific data you've compiled. Think of it as your blueprint for moving forward. Having a tech plan in place will ensure that purchases and decisions made related to technology in the library will have a strategic value or impact; some interpret it as a way to avoid superfluous spending. A tech plan will also all but guarantee alignment with the library's strategic plan, which will be a future step. (See appendix A for a sample technology plan.)

TechSoup for Libraries (n.d.-a) suggests starting the creation of a tech plan with a tech inventory and assessment. The inventory portion involves just that, taking inventory of what hardware and software your library owns, while the assessment goes more in depth and should be a comprehensive look at technology processes in your institution, from staffing to purchasing to budget. Both the inventory and the assessment will provide valuable information on where to best spend your money, time, and effort going forward to address your community's needs. TechSoup for Libraries is a fantastic free online resource to help guide you through this process. It walks you through step by step, starting with your mission and vision and going through budget, policies, training, and evaluation. This can be an especially helpful resource because of the way it logically takes you through the process, starting with the big picture ideas and slowly working its way down to the specifics and budget line items.

Once the inventory and assessment are finished, you are ready for big picture thinking. Analyze all of your data thus far, including your community research and your tech inventory and assessment. At this point you may find gaps or areas to improve, which is your desired outcome; this will allow you to better serve your community over time. (If you are having trouble finding areas to improve, do not fret! Some strategies to help identify those are discussed in the next section.) Improving upon these gaps may involve articulating specific goals such as increasing Internet speed, developing a library app, exploring professional level software suites, and hiring and maintaining technology specialist staff. Tech plans are meant to project a path into the future, so do not feel that these are goals you need to accomplish in the next year or even few years. These are simply goals that you would like to work toward. (See chapter 6 for more information on evaluating data and ensuring that you're inciting real improvement and change with your tech plan.)

WHAT PROBLEM CAN WE SOLVE?

A great way to improve and identify your goals is to ask yourself: What is a pressing problem that needs to be solved in my community? Keep this question in mind as you gather and analyze data; the answer to this question will provide you with the best possible services your library can offer. STEM addresses a nationwide problem that needs to be solved: too few college graduates have the science and math degrees that growing industries like Web development seek in entry-level positions. *Forbes* reports that job-seeking ads looking for 3D printing skills increased 103 percent between August

2013 and August 2014 (Columbus, 2014). Piquing interest among youth in the library with a 3D printer demonstration makes for a highly applicable educational opportunity and might help point them toward a lucrative career. While every community has unique needs, STEM skills are quickly becoming a universal requirement in booming industries in the workforce. Using this mind-set, looking into the future, and predicting what skills will be in high demand can help steer you toward highly relevant library offerings.

The digital divide is an issue that all libraries work to resolve. Simple access to computers, printers, and fax machines may be all that your community desires, but finding the balance between fulfilling basic needs and pushing the envelope with technology is one of the many reasons a needs assessment is so necessary.

Arapahoe Libraries conducted a survey in which they asked about how their tech services compared to institutions like the Apple Store and Best Buy. They saw a need in the community to offer free technology troubleshooting services that retailers do for a fee, and they wanted to determine whether they could meet that need. The responses indicated that Arapahoe Libraries' patrons already saw the library as a destination for technology help with results that were comparable to those from similar paid services. This gave the library confidence that a team of paraprofessional technology specialists would be a smart investment, as the library likely had room to expand and succeed. It also indicated that Arapahoe Libraries could provide a free service that some people had been paying for, a fantastic solution to a problem.

Another helpful way to find out what your community wants is to look at program and event attendance at your library. What are your most popular offerings, and who shows up for programs the most? If craft programs and knitting clubs are well attended, this may clue you in to invest in a craft-themed makerspace. However, keep in mind that this can be a self-fulfilling prophecy; if you never offer teen programs, don't be surprised when your first attempt at teen programming isn't a huge success. Give yourself enough leeway and agility to build that community over time.

One highly successful example of fulfilling a community's specific needs is the Code Louisville initiative. Louisville, Kentucky, has a thriving tech sector, but similar to the STEM issue, employers in the area could not find enough qualified candidates locally for their open job positions. Seeing this was an issue in the area, the Louisville Free Public Library collaborated with local nonprofits and employers to implement the Code Louisville initiative (Chant, 2015).

First, the library subscribed to Treehouse, a coding education platform that can be used from home or in the library with a library card. With the help of its partners, the library also hosted 12-week training courses to develop the skills needed to enter Louisville's tech industry. As a result, Louisville has bolstered its community and helped underrepresented populations get a foot in the door for tech employment (Chant, 2015). This is a fantastic example of finding the problem in one's community and utilizing library resources to solve it.

STEM programs and Code Louisville certainly address issues that libraries can help solve on a macro basis, but other problems to be solved in the community may be much smaller. Baker & Taylor helped give a grant to a rural library for the purchase of DVDs because the local video store had closed, and Internet speeds in the area were not sufficient for video streaming. Given the situation, the panel felt this was the most cost-efficient solution to provide this community with access to films.

The problem in your community may not always be as obvious as these examples, but that's why community needs assessment, demographic data collection, and brainstorming about problems are so important. You want to maximize community engagement and eventual happiness with tech services in the library. Going into this process with an open mind and the idea that you aren't looking for places where you're failing, but rather places where your library might make a real difference, can help library staff have a positive attitude about the potential future changes and will go a long way toward earning their engagement and excitement overall.

ALIGNING WITH YOUR STRATEGIC PLAN

Once you have the information about your community's needs and have identified some problems to solve, improvements to make, and goals to reach, you can integrate your ideas into your library's strategic plan. Whether formalized or not, every library generally has a strategic plan that helps guide the library's mission and helps decide where to spend finite energy and resources. The good news is that the process of making a tech plan as described above generally aligns your tech and information technology (IT) services with the library's strategic plan.

TechSoup for Libraries (n.d.-b) explains well why it is necessary to align one's tech plan with the library's strategic plan. Having the two work in tandem helps prevent getting caught up in irrelevant factors, like wanting to invest in a device because it excites the people with the budget money rather than being a worthy investment for your library patrons. It can be easy to forget the scope of your library's mission in the heat of the moment, and bringing the tech plan and strategic plan together can help ensure making smart investments for your staff and community. For example, gadgets and 3D printers are great to see in libraries, especially for tech-focused initiatives, but you also need to adhere to the philosophy that these have to be integrated into a strategy for the library rather than blindly purchased because they are trendy.

Considering this book's emphasis on going further with technology in libraries, you will want to find ways to bolster your tech services and accomplish your goals. This may involve a different interpretation of the strategic plan, if not a change to it altogether. Since strategic plans most often help those in charge prioritize important services, you may want to use this book and the resources provided (not to mention the data you gather) to demonstrate to your superiors that technology services need to be a priority. A combination of hard, tangible numbers and evidence to illustrate successes, along with the occasional story or anecdote to support them, will help your superiors envision what you are asking for. Some people react most to appeals to their emotions, like heartwarming stories. Some people react best to hard, logical evidence, such as statistics or charts and graphs. Cover all of your bases and weave together the most convincing pitch. Once you have the backing of the library's strategic plan, it is only a matter of time and work to start improving your technology services.

AFFORDABLE ALTERNATIVES

Fortunately much of the community needs assessment can be done in-house. There are plenty of firms and professionals that can be brought into your community to perform a needs assessment, but since this chapter's recommendations largely rely on volunteers getting into the community and asking questions, an in-house effort is ideal both for cost savings and for the purposes of this plan. Of course, staff time and energy are expendable resources, and this cost is likely to be lower overall than hiring external firms. Volunteers are ideal for data collection, and the only cost involved is taking the time to educate volunteers about the library's offerings.

The data-gathering resources referred to in this chapter are all free, most using census data and government resources. Though this chapter discourages relying solely on a survey, a survey is certainly better than nothing. A free survey can be created using Survey Monkey, which is a pretty powerful tool, allowing for Likert-style survey methods (meaning "strongly agree" to "strongly disagree" ratings for various questions) or simple written answers. In light of the response bias you are likely to encounter with an in-library survey, try to at least make an effort to find survey respondents outside the library walls, such as setting up a table at the local recreation center or county fair or posting an ad on Craigslist.

Much of the rest of a needs assessment is simply staff time. For example, finding the need in your community might involve embedding yourself in community gatherings or going to town hall meetings. Otherwise, much of the needs assessment is research heavy, and you wouldn't imagine a library would have any issue finding the time or staff to help with some research! Assigning a reference librarian or two to do an initial assessment, then building upon that, would be a fantastic and low-risk way to begin a successful needs assessment. From there you might put together a committee of staff members from all over the organization to discuss and interpret some of these data and results.

3

Technology-Specialized Staff

- Why Tech-Specialized Employees?
- Tech Specialist Staff
- Staffing and Staff Considerations
- Hiring Tech Specialists
- Retention and Supervision
- Learning and Development
- Complications Regarding Tech Specialist Staff
- Affordable Alternatives

WHY TECH-SPECIALIZED EMPLOYEES?

Chapter 1 laid out the groundwork for why libraries need to raise the bar when it comes to technology services. The next logical step is to look at how to implement those higher level tech services. This chapter focuses on staffing considerations: what's going on now with library staff, how to recruit and maintain a great tech-focused team, and how to coach and train staff to be their best.

Literacy can be defined in a number of ways, all of which can be relevant to multiple library specialties (Steele, 2014). Today, librarians and talented library staff are needed more than ever, but the way we define success and the way we deliver services to patrons have evolved. As a result, staffing needs have evolved. Literacy means being conversant in a number of media, not just the ability to read or write in a particular language, but also the ability to effectively use technology and new media (Steele, 2014).

To succeed in today's fast-evolving, tech-centric library environment, library employees need to utilize the same skills and philosophies that they always have but apply them in a different manner. It is not just tech needs that require staff to be flexible, but also new uses of library space. For example, today it is not uncommon to see "quiet rooms" in public libraries rather than maintaining the expectation of quietness throughout the library. With the ubiquity of Google and search engines in everyday life, a new challenge is added to reference work because many patrons expect that everything can be found immediately with a quick search. Much as the needs of library patrons have changed, the competencies and requirements of successful library staff have changed.

Despite these changes, demand for help from library staff remains as high as ever. According to a 2012 Pew study of library services in the digital age, half of the visitors to the library in the previous year had visited to get help from a librarian (Zickuhr, Rainie, & Purcell, 2013). In addition, libraries have become tech hubs: places for library patrons to access the Internet either with a personal device or on a public computer. If patrons are visiting the library for help from a librarian and so many are utilizing the Internet and public computers at the library, what do those interactions involve on the part of the librarian?

Statistics imply that those interactions are not reference related, which The Institute of Museum and Library Services defines as "an information contact that involves the knowledge, use, recommendations, interpretation, or instruction in the use of one or more information sources by a member of the library staff" (2014). In other words, reference is what some might think of as a traditional librarian's role, connecting people with information and resources. In 2012 the institute reported a nearly 4 percent decrease in reference transactions from the previous year (IMLS, 2014). Since studies show that library patrons still visit the library for help from a librarian, these numbers correlate with the idea that patrons are asking library staff less for traditional reference information and more for other types of help. Some 76 percent of libraries surveyed in 2012 reported that staff had helped patrons fill out an online job application in the past year, an increase of 10 percent from the previous year (American Library Association, 2014). Taking these findings with what we now know about the increase in Wi-Fi usage and digital resource circulation in libraries, there's a high likelihood that an increasing number, perhaps even the majority, of interactions with library staff are technology related.

Despite the uptick in technology questions, the same report stated that nearly half of the libraries surveyed reported insufficient staff or staff knowledge to provide help with e-government forms (ALA, 2012). An e-government form can be any type of online form for taxes, citizenship, or other important services. There are a number of possibilities to account for the findings of this report: e-government forms could represent a longer interaction than the library employee could tackle at the time, there could have been technology troubleshooting difficulties involved with the interactions, or the libraries could simply be understaffed. What this does suggest, however, is that library staff felt unprepared for these tech-related questions.

The increased desire to access e-resources in libraries can help explain the increase in tech interactions and the decrease in reference interactions. One librarian's observation was that there was a shift in questions once downloadable e-book services such as Overdrive had been established and popularized. She observed that the majority of questions were related to e-books or Web site issues. The librarian also reported that a large portion of library staff time was now spent on helping library patrons with e-books and that technology support was becoming more common (Zickuhr, Rainie, Purcell, Madden, & Brenner, 2012). This librarian summarizes the change in patron behavior that was seen in many libraries. As Overdrive and other third-party e-content providers became well-utilized services, library patrons came into their local libraries with a reasonable expectation: that the library employees could help them navigate these new formats.

This shift in patron needs also posed another challenge that library employees had not previously encountered. Many of the third-party e-content providers launched with convoluted, confusing steps for downloading and accessing the content. Further causing issues was that the process was different for each device and medium. All of a sudden, library employees were expected to know the ins and outs of a variety of tablets and devices, to be able to interface with a multitude of passwords and content providers, and to know what the heck DRM (digital rights management) stood for. As time wore on and e-content circulated more and more, it became clear that these third-party providers were expanding while retaining their complexities, so libraries and library employees would need to become even more tech literate to keep up with patron demand.

This sudden demand for tech knowledge in staff does not always overlap with already existing librarian skills; a superstar reference librarian may not necessarily be comfortable with e-content, devices, and technology troubleshooting. Or a staff member may be especially conversant with Android devices but doesn't own any Apple devices and is intimidated when asked about iPads. This is certainly not to say that librarians and library employees have not been able to rise to the challenge and evolve with patrons' tech needs; it simply means that moving forward, technology skills are more of a hiring priority than in the past.

Library Journal published an article by Wilder in 2013 that illustrates this priority. The author notes that the current state of libraries has essentially made technologists out of everyone, requiring more knowledge of technology troubleshooting and technology tool use in general. There is less need for what Wilder calls lower skilled employees, those who handle physical materials and basic circulation interactions. The current environment of libraries has made tech skills more desirable, and patron behavior drives that trend. If a larger audience is using the library's Web site, it only makes sense to bolster the staff who contribute content or work on the technical portion of it.

An Alaskan librarian summed up this divide between the skills of old and the need for the new. She felt that she was not trained to troubleshoot technology, but she was trained to lead library patrons toward resources on technology ("Is Tech Support Professional Work?," 2009). There is a gray area between treating an interaction like a reference question and actually troubleshooting something on the spot as tech support would. On the other hand, an article on trends in libraries by Nancy Bolt (n.d.) posits that there should be no gray area, that librarians need to be the tech support for their community, and that it is not only the IT department's responsibility anymore. There is a need for IT staff to maintain servers, update computers, and make technology purchases. Libraries also need library staff to field questions, host programs, and do front-facing work. However, taking the current environment into consideration, it would seem that an intersection between the two would serve library communities well.

TECH SPECIALIST STAFF

A combination of IT and library staff, a staff member who understands and is able to skillfully utilize technology while understanding library policy and customer service, ideally solves the current staffing issues: staff unpreparedness, the time to answer complex tech questions, and the ability to teach technology literacy to both staff and patrons. These staff members, often referred to as technology specialists, are an essential addition to the current library environment.

Tech specialists spend the majority of their time on the library floor helping library patrons with technology via walk-ups, classes, or appointments. They are generally meant to be able to help with more complex technology interactions, perhaps ones that will take longer to solve or are simply more demanding. Depending on the size of the library or the volume of technology questions, they may also help out with basic interactions. Their other responsibilities vary by system, but it is not uncommon for technology specialist staff to deliver programs and help with outreach as well.

At Arapahoe Libraries, technology specialists quickly became the hottest commodity on staff. Tech staff walk into busier branches for their shifts to find lines of several people all awaiting their help. Staff and patrons frequently ask when hours can be expanded. The online comment form is inundated with glowing reviews and descriptions of technology specialists patiently solving problems and teaching along the way. It is not even necessarily the case that generalist library staff had not been able to solve these issues previously; they just were not as available because they had to keep their time freed up for basic short interactions like paying fines and placing holds.

Before there were technology specialist staff members at libraries, the stopgap measure for many was one-on-one appointments. As a result, staff were not able to help patrons at that moment with their problems, and these appointments were often booked for days later. This scenario did not provide the best possible customer service for patrons or make it easy for staff who had to break the news to a patron with a time-sensitive issue that he or she would have to wait to have the question answered. In the past, when was it appropriate for a librarian at a reference desk to turn away a query to be answered at a later date? With technology specialists on staff, more likely than not someone is available soon or immediately for any tech issues, and waiting days or even a week for help is no longer the norm.

Over time tech specialist staff at Arapahoe Libraries have been able to increase the frequency and complexity of technology questions fielded (see appendix B). Since the service was new, it took time for library patrons to learn about it and to bring their devices and troubleshooting needs to technology specialists. Since then, due to word of mouth, marketing, and space design (see chapter 4 for more information), the frequency of such requests has grown enough to justify more technology specialist staff hours. Similarly, early on basic tablet questions and printing help were the norm. Dealing with e-content downloading issues and providing help with them were also common. Now, while those types of questions still come through the library doors, 3D design, challenging laptop issues, and Web site design questions have also become frequent. Technology-specialized staff have been able to not only solve the existing needs of the library and community, but further justify their existence by expanding to those who may not have known the library offered the more in-depth and extensive tech help they were seeking.

STAFFING AND STAFF CONSIDERATIONS

There are a variety of ways that a technology specialist team can be put together. An early iteration of the technology specialist idea at Arapahoe Libraries was to position tech liaisons at each branch of the library system. Their duties were similar to that of a tech specialist, though they were not united under one department or supervisor. Without a unified purpose or clearly defined mission, their work slowly returned to general rather than specialized, often falling into the same roles that they had before. There were a few pitfalls that were avoided in future iterations. Some of the liaisons were part time, and without the removal or reprioritization of their other responsibilities, adding tech competencies left them with little or no time to improve or delve deeper into that specialty.

Many libraries have used a specialized tech librarian or some specialist technology staff member as a stopgap measure, finding that there is a need for this skill in their libraries. Although this is not a one-size-fits-all solution, having a department or team of technology specialists that can trade skills and ideas or even build a knowledge base is often the ideal and most lasting way to address patron needs consistently and efficiently.

The team can be formed from scratch or from existing library staff. Using existing staff of course is the more budget-friendly consideration, but keep in mind that the right technology specialist job postings can attract applicants with a range of differing technology skills that can be very exciting to offer. It is not uncommon for teams of technology specialists to include engineers, scientists, musicians, artists, and graphic designers. The public opinion of libraries and library jobs is so positive that a creative and challenging technology specialist job can seem appealing even to those who have a high earning potential, above what most libraries can offer. There are trained engineers on tech specialist teams who have chosen to work at the library out of passion rather than the pursuit of the almighty dollar.

HIRING TECH SPECIALISTS

When hiring technology specialists, there are several considerations to keep in mind. A variety of individuals with all kinds of backgrounds and skill sets are likely to apply. Library science degree holders, IT workers, and artists are just a small sample, and there are specific considerations when hiring from each group. As mentioned previously in this chapter, there are excellent reasons to separate IT work and library staff work. Therefore, applicants with IT backgrounds do not tend to be the best individuals to hire, for fear they may prioritize back-end technology upkeep over technology-related customer service.

Having a library science degree does not necessarily define an ideal technology specialist. Individuals with library science degrees are great! They are all but guaranteed to have the library philosophy and basic library work down pat. However, *requiring* a library science degree for a tech specialist job, either paraprofessional or professional, is not recommended, because it excludes a broad range of applicants with amazing technology skills. Having a few different specializations within the team, like someone who excels at graphic design and someone who loves tinkering with and fixing the 3D printer, makes for the widest possible tech skill set to offer your patrons. Especially if you have an appointment system, being able to point library patrons to the person on your team with a specialty they love and excel at is a crucial factor in having the best possible team. There are plenty of tech-savvy library science degree holders out there, so keeping your search for the perfect tech specialist broad is ideal. (For a good example, see the Denver Public Library's posting for a "Technology Specialist—Community Technology Center" at http://agency.governmentjobs.com/denverlibrary/job_bulletin.cfm?jobID=1264311&sharedWindow=0.)

Although specializing tech skills on your tech team is ideal, hiring for fit, personality, willingness to learn, and customer service skills should be prioritized over hiring for existing tech knowledge. Teaching an individual tech skills is preferable to hiring a tech-savvy person who does not have people skills. A highly qualified graphic designer who knows her or his way around the entire Adobe Creative Suite is a tempting applicant, but if she or he cannot translate those skills into a friendly learning opportunity for a library patron, those skills are useless in our public-facing workplace. Therefore, in the job interview, look first for people skills rather than tech skills. Existing tech knowledge is a huge plus, but not a necessity to work on a technology specialist team. Ask questions such as the following:

- One day, a library patron comes in asking you for help with software you aren't comfortable or familiar with. How would you handle the situation?
- Tell us about a new technology that interests you. How do you keep up with tech trends?

These interview questions help vet not the amount of tech knowledge, but the applicant's relationship with technology. Note that these questions do not imply that existing tech skills are expected; the questions are meant to find out about the way the person *interacts with* technology. Is the applicant afraid of being asked a question about technology she or he does not know about? If so, that person probably would not make a great technology specialist, as learning on the fly and in front of library patrons can be a daily occurrence. Seeing what technology the applicant is interested in helps us suss out what she or he might be passionate about, might specialize in. Applicants' answers tell us if they are tech geeks who tinker for fun or if they are more casual users of technology; both can become great employees.

When hiring technology specialist staff in libraries, it is crucial to keep your eye out for, and avoid hiring, "mansplainers." While there are a number of women and men highly qualified to work as technology specialists, there are also tech-savvy men out there who do not listen to or are not comfortable with tech-savvy women. As a result, they tend to talk down to women, adopting a legitimate or feigned expertise to explain the issue or subject. These men assume talented women are unaware of or unable to comprehend complex technology interactions unless they are explained to them by a male authority. Considering that 80 percent of all library workers are women, and the majority of all library card holders are women, a technology specialist with these tendencies would quickly become an ineffective, unpleasant employee to work with and learn from (American Library Association, 2014; Department for Professional Workers, AFL-CIO, 2011).

To combat these condescending attitudes, filtering questions such as the following might give you an idea about an applicant's tendency toward this behavior and could at least make that person aware that the organization is not tolerant of this unequal treatment.

- What challenges do women, especially those in technology-focused fields, face in today's workplace?
- Part of your responsibility as a tech specialist would be to learn and demonstrate technologies such as 3D printing to the average, perhaps less

tech-savvy, library patron. Give us an example of a time you demystified technology for someone.

In the interview itself, consider having a female coworker sit in; observing how an applicant communicates with a male interviewer as compared to a female interviewer can be telling. You are also nonverbally communicating to the applicant that this technology department is not a "boy's club," that women in this specialty in the organization are valued. The specific question about women's issues in the workplace communicates to the applicant that there are issues to be considered about the inequalities facing women in tech-related fields. In the best interviews, the applicant demonstrates an investment or an interest in the issue, noting that it is a frequent enough occurrence to justify interview questions. The person's answer and empathy regarding the issue usually tell the interviewer how the applicant would treat and talk to women. Delving deeper, hearing the applicant's strategy for explaining complex technology to someone, both tells the interviewer how she or he would be as a teacher and exemplifies the person's ability to educate an individual of any sex or race in an equal manner.

Once the technology specialist team has been put together, the challenge comes to the supervisor. How do you cultivate a smart, loyal, happy team? There's an oft-cited statement that the number one reason employees leave is to get away from their bosses (Weber, 2015). There is definitely truth to that. From a tech specialist supervisor's perspective, the key to keeping staff is autonomy. A lot of informal learning and tinkering has to happen to foster a successful tech specialist. There are many things to learn and many opportunities to learn them. Many small, fun, tech-related projects can crop up. Maybe a staff member asks: Can we try a promotional projector screen in the library and run it on a Raspberry Pi? Being a boss who allows for autonomy, you trust your employee to try that project and learn about microcontrollers like the Raspberry Pi in the process. Tinkering is an important part of learning the plethora of technology that this job can entail. A boss who allows for flexibility is a necessity.

Of course, it can't hurt to ask! Out and out saying that autonomy is common in the job and that the supervisor expects self-motivated projects certainly drives the point home:

> This job allows for creativity and autonomy; your supervisor will encourage lots of personal projects and specialization. Tell us about a time when you were self-motivated at work.

This sets the expectation from the interviewer that the job requires autonomy, and the creativity of the applicant's example, the way she or he has found work in a past job, is revealing.

Finding Great Technology Trainers

During the hiring process, you are primarily looking for friendly people who instill you with confidence that they can teach well. This section provides a few tips about what to look for in the interview process and what standards to hold your staff to. There are many ways in which a technology specialist at the library can educate library patrons. One of the most important qualities of any tech specialist is her or his ability to explain. In interviews, it is not uncommon to pass up incredibly tech-savvy applicants because they seem to lack the ability to educate others with their knowledge. There is no science to this, especially in a 30-minute interview, but if the applicant makes assumptions about what the interviewers' existing tech knowledge is, this is usually a telltale sign that the individual may not be able to disseminate information in a digestible format. Often applicants see "technology" in the job description and assume a depth of tech knowledge is all that's needed. Educators and individuals who have volunteered or worked for nonprofits tend to be best suited to this job, partially due to their empathy, passion for helping others, and/or background in teaching.

Gerding (2007) rightfully emphasizes that enthusiasm, charisma, and soft skills tend to be more ideal than tech savvy in an ideal trainer. Some people may frequently be bored to tears by teaching a basic class on using a mouse or Microsoft Office, so enthusiasm for helping people learn is far more important than preexisting knowledge on the subject. Being welcoming in the classroom is key to creating a great environment. When someone enters your makerspace, employees should introduce themselves and ask the entrant's name to immediately establish a friendly, personal basis. Steps like this break down any hesitancy the learner might have. A sense of humor can also create a positive classroom environment. Gerding (2007) encourages and repeatedly asks for "stupid questions" throughout the classes she teaches. This eases the tension of having to ask in front of one's peers a question that the learner might fear has an obvious answer, when in fact it is likely that the same question is on many minds!

RETENTION AND SUPERVISION

An important consideration is that technology specialists, especially those hired externally, are highly employable. Passionate individuals with impressive skill sets are attracted to these library jobs and tend to have the type of résumé that can be applicable and attractive to many fields. Though hiring supervisors are sometimes content to "rent" a great employee for a year before losing that person rather than keeping an average employee for too long, retention makes for a better team. As indicated by one of the sample interview questions, one way to keep employees is to allow for some creativity and autonomy in the job. These highly skilled individuals often grow passionate about libraries and have many ideas they want to implement. The best thing a supervisor can do is allow these ideas to grow organically and to remove as many roadblocks to their success as possible. If an employee's ideas are consistently squashed or shot down, she or he is more likely to seek out an employer who will be more accepting of those ideas.

A public library will never be able to compensate an individual with a strong graphic design background or engineering degree as well as a commercial entity could. But few other employers can offer the satisfaction of providing free (or nearly free) and fantastic technology help. When selling potential applicants on the job, make it a point to say that a technology specialist's job is to connect people with technology, not to sell them anything. This tends to resonate with prospective applicants who have come from a background of retail or other commercial business.

LEARNING AND DEVELOPMENT

One of the most crucial parts of tech specialist development is scheduling a regularly occurring time during which the specialists can learn new technology. At Arapahoe Libraries, it's called tinker time. Tinker time happens once weekly in the early morning hours on Sunday, before the library is open. It is held in the library's makerspace or media lab, a location that allows for plenty of creative risk-taking with technology. Although learning on the fly is a necessity of being a technology specialist, providing a private and quiet environment in which employees can delve deeply into what they are learning is a good idea. Tinker time allows technology specialist staff to expand their knowledge and become better and more confident in their skills. In some cases, this time can be formalized a bit with skill shares from the tech staff, quick tutorials or once-overs of a tech issue they have recently encountered or a demonstration of a skill they are especially adept at. A similar skill-share model can be used for development days or trainings to help train and engage all library staff.

Technology specialist staff need to be willing to learn on the fly and to admit when they do not know how to do something. This especially falls in line with the ideal hiring philosophy that a great technology specialist does not necessarily need to be an expert in coding, Web development, or graphic design on day one. However, in the library's mission to raise awareness and attract higher level technology questions and more complex interactions, it often falls to the technology specialists to offer classes, demos, or trainings on something they may not yet be expert in. For example, Denver Public Library patrons had long been requesting a class on the coding language Python, but none of the staff at the Community Technology Center felt capable of teaching it. One of the CTC staff members, Cody, came up with a novel solution to the problem. Since he had trouble lining up an outside instructor, he decided to make the class collaborative. Cody let his attendees know that if they were willing to learn alongside him, he was happy to "teach" the class, reminding them throughout that there was no one expert; everyone was there to help one another. The attendees loved the model, and everyone in the class was able to offer help clarifying confusing steps and troubleshooting pesky errors at various points during the course. The course became much more collaborative than it would have been if an instructor had simply lectured over the course of the classes.

Use this story as inspiration when thinking about teaching technology to others. You could offer a coding camp over the summer using Codecademy's after-school coding program. As long as you stay one or two lessons ahead of the class, no problem. Maybe you could have a graphic design meet-up at which you encourage skill sharing in Photoshop or GIMP. As long as the instructor is ready and willing to not be the expert in the room, and as long as attendees are well aware that the course is collaborative learning and skill sharing rather than a lecture, this is a great way to offer technology classes outside of one's expertise. As a bonus, the second or third time your staff member teaches the class, she or he probably could switch over to a lecture model after becoming familiar with the material. Look for more insight and information on technology classes and teaching in chapter 5.

COMPLICATIONS REGARDING TECH SPECIALIST STAFF

Although hiring and deploying tech specialist staff in libraries is mostly sunshine and rainbows in terms of the positives outweighing the negatives, there are a few considerations to keep in mind when following this path. One pitfall of having specialized staff, especially tech specialist staff, is the misperception that generalist library staff no longer need to be tech savvy. After all, there's a technology person who can take care of those questions, right? Consider this common scenario. For one reason or another, one library staff member becomes the go-to tech person. Though this is a sound plan, this often occurs to the detriment of staff and patrons. Library patrons can be left waiting for simple interactions like printing a document because the single tech person is occupied. The other staff do not feel comfortable, they simply do not bother to learn, or the tech person is always so busy with these interactions that she or he does not have the time to train other staff (Bertot et al., 2011). It is easy to lose goodwill when the public feels that library staff can't answer questions about the library's resources. To a layperson, a question about her or his specific device should be easy to answer. After all, shouldn't library employees be experts on the resources they offer? Isn't it reasonable to assume that library employees are capable of helping with information that pertains to the library?

Although technology specialization in libraries is the most effective way to expand and improve upon your library's tech offerings, this problem is alarmingly common. The best course of action is to know that this can be a potential outcome before planning a staffing change. Put the technology specialist into a mentor role for other staff members, encourage her or him to educate while solving technology issues and to follow up after an issue is resolved to let the staff member know how to help next time. Implementing basic technology competencies for all staff in performance reviews is another way to ensure that they are not resting on their laurels when it comes to technology skills.

Technology specialists themselves can also be in danger of causing the "guru issue" on their own teams. If someone is an expert on 3D printing and someone is an expert in film editing, naturally one would try to triage questions on those subjects to the appropriate staff member. However, if this happens too often, tech specialists might expose gaps in their knowledge or acquire a fear of a certain type of interaction due to lack of familiarity. It is important for tech specialists to take steps like creating knowledge bases, doing skill shares, and taking on the occasional challenge to create the ideal team of helpers. Tech specialists need to be relatively interchangeable in terms of their knowledge, especially if they are a distributed or large team.

Tiering questions can also help alleviate the tech guru issue among generalist staff and technology specialist staff. Using tiers for reference transactions is fairly common. Houston Public Library piloted the unified service model, which involves three tiers. Tier one questions are answerable by any floor staff member; these can be directional questions or basic reference transactions. Tier two is a more challenging reference transaction, to be elevated to a librarian or remote reference services. Tier three encompasses questions or interactions that cannot be answered with the resources on hand or when the tier two help was not sufficient (Urban Libraries Council, 2012). A similar model can be implemented for use among technology specialist staff.

For example, basic technology interactions, such as connecting a device to Wi-Fi or giving an overview of an e-content provider, should be answerable by any floor staff member. More complex interactions should be passed off by generalists to the tech specialists. Questions like this often include help learning to use a brand new smartphone, learning how to download and access e-content, and fixing a slow computer. Any questions that are not answerable by the tech specialist can be raised to the final tier, which can include a call or visit to the device manufacturer, a referral to another tech specialist who has more familiarity with the issue, or a ticket to the IT department.

This tiered system also makes for the best flow of questions. Technology specialist staff are ideally available for the longer, more complex questions, while the generalist staff can handle the basics. The technology specialist staff can be thought of as mostly hands on, while generalist staff are mostly hands off. Generalist staff can describe and suggest e-content providers and find titles. Technology specialist staff can help patrons open an account and troubleshoot any issues along the way.

An important consideration with tiered questions is the reference interview. Any library employee should be well versed in asking probing questions to help answer patrons' inquiries, but this can fall by the wayside in the tiering system. After technology specialist staff are established, library patrons may begin to ask for their help specifically. However, it is still important for the generalist staff to probe and ask exactly what the issue is, because it may be a question they can answer themselves. If generalist staff get used to automatically passing off any question or interaction that involves a laptop, device, or the word "technology," they will become too reliant on technology specialist staff and deprive themselves of learning on their own.

The relationship with the IT department plays an important role in implementing technology specialist staff. There can sometimes be a bit of a struggle between the two, and it is necessary to delineate which tasks are whose. The technology specialist staff want to improve the patron experience, while the IT department needs to keep everything running smoothly and consistently for staff and the public. And as the Alaskan librarian cited previously mentioned, library staff should not necessarily be used just as tech support. However, in today's library environment, it is unrealistic to expect IT staff to help with all patron-specific technology issues. One reason is that today's library environment has so much more tech available to patrons beyond the basic public computers, Internet, and printers that were the main responsibilities of IT in the past. Faster Wi-Fi, projectors, self-checkout stations, computers for children, content kiosks and vending machines, and maintaining third-party content provider software are only a handful of common resources in libraries that IT generally oversees. In light of these responsibilities, IT should be able to focus on them, along with preventive maintenance.

Allowing IT to focus on those issues while the technology specialists focus on the patron-facing issues makes for the best patron experience on both sides. An example of where problems can crop up is a lack of administrative access to patron computers or wireless issues. Patrons naturally assume that the technology specialist should be able to fix slow Internet speeds or install a necessary update on a patron computer, but these are usually tasks left to the IT department. Though it might be tempting to give technology specialist staff administrative rights on the computers and other IT-related systems in the library, this is likely to lead to a technology specialist having to balance patron-facing customer service interactions with tech maintenance in the library as opposed to being able to simply focus on a good customer service experience. A better relationship between tech specialists and IT is to have the tech specialists serve as the frontline defense who can solve simple technology issues in the library and send in detailed tickets to IT when they come across an issue they cannot solve. This can even lead to an IT department that can be proactive rather than reactive in solving tech issues in the library. A hybrid IT/tech specialist may be a good compromise for a library on a smaller budget, but we have found it is ideal to keep the two separate. Above all, maintaining a positive, communicative relationship between these two groups is crucial to curating a successful technology specialist team.

AFFORDABLE ALTERNATIVES

After a presentation on technology specialist staff at a local conference, a participant asked a deflating question: "How do you expect all libraries to afford to pay these engineers and graphic designers you have on hand?" The presentation was heavy on details about the amazing individuals who were interested in being on Arapahoe Libraries' technology specialist team and the uptick in patron satisfaction and question complexity. Indeed, Arapahoe Libraries are able to pay a decent wage, albeit not one that rivals an engineer's salary. All libraries on all budgets cannot realistically attract and afford this type of tech specialist staff. That said, many of these talented individuals were attracted to the job not for the financial reward, but for the passion of connecting the community with technology and sharing their sought-after skills.

However, if hiring and paying a team of unique individuals of this caliber is not possible on your budget, don't despair. Many libraries have technology volunteers or have reworked existing jobs in the library to be more tech focused. At Library 21C in Colorado Springs, the business librarian is also the laser cutter expert in the makerspace. Arapahoe Libraries could likely have created a successful technology specialist team by hiring completely internally or tweaking existing jobs to help with the new demand; the process would have simply been more training intensive. Although specialization is ideal for technology help, combining responsibilities in this way can help stretch your staffing budget further.

Cupertino Library had the same issue that many libraries face: an increasing demand for e-reader and device help and reference librarians who were not equipped with the time or the knowledge to deal with it. Instead of hiring technology specialist staff or creating that new job within their organization, they put in the volunteer-run Tech Toolbar, a point of contact in the library that is staffed during peak hours to help library patrons with mobile devices. There are also a number of tablets and devices on hand for the volunteers to demonstrate on (Urban Libraries Council, 2013). As a result, Cupertino Library was able to fulfill the same community need with volunteers and a onetime cost of purchasing devices rather than the long-term expense of hiring staff. Similarly, the Community Technology Center at Denver Public Library would never have been able to keep up with its 100 plus public computers, one-on-one appointments, and computer classes without a stable of fantastic volunteers to help fill the gaps. Your job is to find the right balance among paid staff, volunteers, and your budget.

Another avenue to explore to find people with technology talents is internships and volunteer opportunities. Denver is home to Galvanize, a tech startup that offers Web development boot camps with job placement afterward. Galvanize is often looking for sponsors to help place graduates of the program. Asking a graduate to teach a coding class or to intern on the library's IT or Web team could mirror some of the outcomes of a tech specialist team. The coding and development community has a number of initiatives to help nonprofits create Web sites or to help educate underserved communities, and involving them or partnering them with the library is another possibility for tech growth.

4

Space Design and Marketing

The next logical step in developing customer-facing tech services for your library is to consider space design and marketing. Take into account what the services will look like in action in the library and how people will find out about them. Having already collected and considered information about community needs and staffing, you should have what you need for the next step.

SPACE DESIGN ASSESSMENT

Start with the space. First, take a look at your library. Where do the most tech questions originate? Do you want a technology desk behind the reference desk? Maybe in or near your makerspace? The best location isn't always the most obvious place, like closest to the public computers. In some communities a high number of library patrons bring in their own devices looking for help, so an easily found desk near the front is a better location than near the public computers. Your floor staff will have useful information on this.

Especially in roving reference models, staff get to know the "hot spots" where patrons tend to have the most questions.

In the field of space design and architecture, this type of thinking is known as *zoning*. The process of zoning helps architects and planners decide where things should be laid out for maximum comfort and efficiency. In a library context, the often loud children's and teens' areas are best located farther away from the more traditionally quiet reference or public computer areas. Other library branches have lots of printing needs, so a tech desk with line of sight to that area might be important. In some branches, maybe you want to demonstrate technology, so staying away from the quieter areas would be ideal so as not to disturb people with the sounds and sights of these demos.

Whenever possible, maintaining line of sight with the first staffed point of service in the library is paramount. This is important for two reasons. First, this enables the easiest possible handoffs from generalist staff; the technology specialist is always a short walk away. Second, this placement allows the technology specialist to jump in when a line forms at the front desk. In libraries with multiple services on multiple floors, it may be best to keep the tech desk near the main entrance and the front desk for this very reason. Although a tech specialist's primary function is to solve technology questions, jumping in to provide extra help is only reasonable. The alternative would seem like bad customer service, turning patrons away or making them wait longer when help is needed. Depending on the size of your library, staffed technology desks on multiple floors may be best suited to your situation.

Furniture and placement choices may seem insignificant, but they communicate the type and friendliness of service in your space. A large reference desk hiding a librarian behind it is far less approachable than a smaller desk with a chair for the patron to pull up (Mathews & Soistmann, 2016). One says "the librarian has the answer, wait in front of the desk to get it," while the other says "pull up a chair and let's find this answer together." Similarly, large monitors that hide line of sight to the tech specialist's face make staff less approachable and hinder their ability to be proactive and friendly to passersby. Many libraries embrace the roving reference model, which asks that staff get out from behind the desk and approach library patrons to see if they need help. This model may not work for a technology specialist desk; a more static service point is better. A static service point helps to solidify that location as the place to go for tech help. After some time, patrons will learn that the technology desk is the place to go for complex tech help, while the other desks are for more general library help. Therefore, be sure to avoid the fortress-like reference desks of old and consider smaller, slimmer points of contact with less furniture between staff and the patron.

There are some questions specific to a technology space to consider. Do you plan to teach computer classes? Is there space and privacy for one-on-one appointments? If so, you might consider a computer classroom or study rooms near your technology desk or near public computers. Are the copier, scanner, and printers all located near the public computers or the technology desk area? These are common computer-related needs that a technology specialist can help with. Is IT in the building? Is the area nearby or readily accessible for easy handoffs if necessary? Is there ample space for personal devices, and are there plugs to charge them and Ethernet ports for those who want a wired connection? Try to anticipate as many of these considerations as possible before making any irreversible furniture or location decisions.

Accessibility

Accessibility should also be taken into consideration when designing a technology space. For example, larger laptop screens are preferable; patrons with poor eyesight have a hard time seeing the steps a technology specialist takes on her or his laptop when troubleshooting or demonstrating. Therefore, a large monitor or even a television mirroring the staff member's computer screen is a useful tool for a technology help space.

When considering these issues, remember that the American with Disabilities Act (1990) dictates that desk height be between 28 and 34 inches above the floor (U.S. Department of Justice, 2010). Adjustable standing desks are a good compromise, as users can move the work surface to the most comfortable height depending on the situation. If you are willing to take it a step further, look beyond ADA standards and embrace universal design. Universal design is a design philosophy that takes into account the largest possible number of accessibility needs and ties them all together to work for every user equally. The thinking behind this is that ADA standards might dictate a wheelchair ramp or ideal counter height here and there, but universal design can inspire the architecture of your entire space or building to be maximally accessible for everyone (West, 2011).

Within the field of technology, there are a number of ways to improve accessibility. Using the zoom-in keyboard shortcut (CTRL and + key on most PCs) is practically a day one back pocket tool to help solve sight issues with small computer screens. The text itself can also be easily made larger on almost any computer, and brightness can be increased or decreased. Many devices have accessibility options for those who lack dexterity with small buttons. You might consider investing in accessible keyboards with larger keys, styluses for touch screens, and magnifiers for your library when these needs come up. Anticipating accessibility needs of your patrons will ensure a smooth launch of the service and, more important, happy users!

Creating a Dedicated Technology Space

Of course you can create a space that fits the community and fill it with technology specialist staff. Business-friendly areas equipped with videoconferencing equipment and meeting space might be the best way to serve your community, and even better, technology specialists can set up in the space and offer assistance or advice. Media labs featuring audiovisual tools would also be a fantastic space in which to embed a technology specialist, helping people record part of the time but also remaining available for any basic tech questions that come through. Having technology specialists in close proximity to spaces like this can help wordlessly communicate what they can help patrons with.

The central branch of Denver Public Library did just this. Formerly, there were public computers spread out across the seven floors of the large urban library. In an effort to help funnel tech questions to one area, DPL created the Community Technology Center (CTC). The CTC is on the fourth floor and has more than 100 public computers and a makerspace, staffed with technology specialists and volunteers. The CTC serves as the technology center for the entirety of the Denver Public Library system, which encompasses a few dozen smaller neighborhood branches. Since it is unrealistic to have a full-blown technology center in every one of these small branches, the CTC helps the branches coordinate tech curriculum and programming, while the branches refer complex tech questions back to the CTC.

Arapahoe Libraries took nearly the opposite approach. Six of the eight public buildings are regularly staffed with technology specialists. This arrangement presented quite a challenge when launching the service, as space needed to be found for tech-focused points of contact in six distinct branches. These branches were not built with multiple types of staff desks in mind, so the primary challenge lay in finding the space and taking into consideration what would be best for each branch. Since each branch was unique, and it took much trial and error to find the sweet spot, temporary desks like rolling laptops were ideal to start with. This way, if a spot did not work, tech specialists were not confined to that particular area. The team discovered that it took quite a bit of time and effort to establish a brand new point of contact and made some mistakes along the way. (Here's a tip: don't put a desk directly behind a support column that blocks line of sight to the front desk!) Only after spending time testing out various spots should you put in a more permanent desk.

There are also a number of creative spaces that can be built for technology staff to curate. The Labs at DC Public Library are a series of different tools and spaces within its Washington, D.C., library. The Labs feature a makerspace, a media conversion center, an audiovisual studio, and an entrepreneurial collaborative space. An ever-changing space in your library can provide yet another viable option for space utilization. The Oak Park Public Library in Illinois launched the Idea Box, which has monthly exhibits ranging from pixel art with golf tees to a space reminiscent of a park, bench included, during a cold winter month (Molaro & White, 2015). Having the space and/or the support for a rotating exhibit or enough square footage for multiple maker-inspired areas may be outside of your scope, but keep in mind this nimble attitude for potential uses of space for tech services.

Using Retail Models as Inspiration

Figuring out ideal patron points of contact for tech services does not have to involve complex research. Instead, take inspiration from existing retail models. Although you may not be able to use every idea in its entirety due to certain key differences between retail and library environments, the retail model is surprisingly adaptable.

Technology services at Best Buy and the Apple Store provide the most applicable examples. Both stores have generalist staff on the floor to help with basic questions and tier two staff who help with more complex needs. At Best Buy, the tier two staff are the Geek Squad; at the Apple Store the staff are the Geniuses. In both cases, the tier two staff have well-labeled points of contact that are clearly different from any other customer service points. Customers have the choice of either coming straight to the tier two point of contact or being handed off by a tier one generalist.

There are some retail model designs that can be applied to tech services at the library. A separate desk is crucial; patrons need to be able to see where they should go for tech help and where to go for a new library card or to ask about a hold. The tech desk needs to look different from the other points of contact to visually communicate to your library patrons that a different type of help happens at that desk.

Finally, big box stores like Best Buy provide easy navigation; one can generally see the "Geek Squad" sign from across the store. These differentiated spaces are modeled after a space design concept called the "store-within-a-store" model (Mathews & Soistmann, 2016). You might also have seen a Starbucks inside a grocery store or a small plus-size section in a Forever 21. These spaces are distinct and might have different lighting, staff, and visual cues. These nonverbal design aspects communicate to users that this is a different service point with different products to offer than elsewhere in the building. Think of the space design in the Apple Store. The store itself is generally small enough or open enough visually that one can see where the Genius Bar is located from almost anywhere. The Genius Bar is generally located at the back, making it highly unlikely that any customer would make it that far back without speaking to a tier one staff member first. This keeps the Geniuses from using up their time on basic interactions. Space design dictates these interactions and nonverbally communicates the role of the Genius Bar.

There are also different space design layouts that lend themselves to a certain type of interaction, known as showrooms, studios, boutiques, and salons (Mathews & Soistmann, 2016). A salon is a space best suited for a classroom-type environment, with a number of seats in rows to accommodate, perhaps, a lecturer. Studios are most synonymous with makerspaces, collaborative areas for creative interactions and various office spaces in which to work together. Showrooms and boutiques are probably the best designs for a technology specialist service. A showroom, the most common of which is the Apple Store, is meant to show off a product. Think of the standing height tables and the clean lines of sight to each product, out in the open and ready for the consumer to interact with. A space like this could be fantastic for technology demos hosted by a technology specialist. Boutiques are best for one-on-one interactions; they tend to be for a single purpose, so a "boutique" design for technology help within the library would most likely suit the service best (Mathews & Soistmann, 2016).

Why the Retail Design Resonates

Considering that the Apple Store's retail model is incredibly successful, public libraries would be wise to take a look at why it resonates with so many people. In a *Harvard Business Review* article, former Apple senior vice president of retail operations Ron Johnson discusses what it is about the Apple Store's model that makes it so successful. It isn't just because it stocks popular Apple products like the iPad and Macbooks, because those can be purchased at Amazon for the same price without tax. Customers are actually paying more money for the experience of purchasing items at the Apple Store (Johnson, 2011). Johnson goes on to say that Apple Store staff are not paid on commission, and their goal is for the customer to leave happy, whether with a new Apple device or with a fixed older one.

Johnson's line of reasoning should sound familiar to any librarian. Libraries have the advantage of being just about the most bipartisan institution one can find, and no library staff will pressure patrons into buying anything. This very principle is what gives technology specialists at the library the edge over retail. Although the Genius Bar and Geek Squad offer fantastic services, and whether they are paid on commission or not, they work for a for-profit business. No matter which way you cut it, the end goal is still for that business to be profitable and to sell its services. A tech specialist in the library, while admittedly not equipped with quite the same toolkit to solve technology issues as those retail institutions, will help to the extent of her or his abilities free of charge. The library patron can trust that the advice received was not influenced by money in any way. So in some ways, libraries can take the best of both the for-profit and nonprofit worlds in utilizing a retail layout while retaining the library customer service philosophy.

Gathering Data for Space Design

Taking into consideration some of the retail inspiration for space design, you should also ask your community what they find most important. Many of the same principles from chapter 2 apply here; getting outside the library walls is important to feel out what might benefit the community most in space design. In fact, marketing goes hand in hand with assessment as a way to gauge whether one's community is being properly served (Dowd, 2013). Be sure to take into account the data you have collected from your community needs analysis. More marketing-focused surveys, interviews, and open forums are also all options. Taking inspiration from retail again, try using retail stores as examples in your surveys. List stores likes Barnes and Noble and the Apple Store and ask how easy they are to navigate while shopping (Sullivan, 2013). The results of such a survey can be a great starting point, as these stores offer a relatively universal familiarity, a starting point from which to compare.

Discoveries from this data collection can be eye-opening or can affirm what you already want in a new space. In a community engagement survey, Calgary Public Library found that natural light and a balance between spaces for gathering and space for an ample collection were some of the most important features for their patrons (Hardy & Griebel, 2014). While this sounds natural (of course users prefer natural light, a large collection, and places to meet), data collection puts it into design philosophy terms.

Similarly, after a large local library remodeled its facility in the Denver area, many patrons complained that the library had "gotten rid of all the books." This was partially true, as the library did reduce the collection size, but those materials were removed because they were not circulating. The redesign provided more meeting room space, comfortable seating, and a cafe. The combination of Wi-Fi statistics, door counts, and circulation numbers implied that library patrons were more interested in finding a nice place to sit and meet or use the Wi-Fi. Circulation numbers affirmed that a large physical collection was not in fact what they wanted, at least from the standpoint of actually checking out materials from that collection. Instead, it seems likely that these patrons took issue with the idea of what a library should look like, with rows upon rows of books, as a physical repository of information, not an institution with more of a community center feel. The lesson to learn is that your library patrons may not always have the best idea of exactly what they want, so your own data and their opinions are best equally balanced.

MARKETING YOUR TECH SERVICE

Marketing and space design go hand in hand. Remember how customers shop at the Apple Store not for lower prices but for the experience? The Apple brand has established certain expectations for consumers through marketing, while those expectations are met or exceeded via space design (and great customer service, of course). Space design in a way is in-building marketing, while formal marketing involves finding what separates your service from others. For example, the author feels that technology help at the library is a better, more positive experience than technology help at big box stores. Sussing out bullet points like this is a great start toward finding the most powerful aspects of your service to market.

This thinking process also helps with one of the most common issues in library marketing: far too many things to market. There are so many materials, resources, and programs that libraries offer, it's impossible to market everything effectively. Therefore, aligning the subject of your marketing to a strategic plan or mission statement is key (Dowd, 2013). This should help focus on exactly what needs to be marketed and remove the stress of choosing from the dozens of things that could be marketed. This focus can also coincide with a content calendar, which is a semiregular theme, usually monthly, that marketing efforts can follow. Perhaps May is health and fitness month, during which health and fitness books, databases, and programs are promoted. This can then tie into an overarching mission statement such as "increase engagement and innovation in the community" or "start and maintain local partnerships." Your mission statement should also help guide the material you are marketing to purely benefit the customer (Watson-Lakamp, 2015). After all, you are serving library patrons, and they are the ones who stand to benefit from the service you are marketing.

Taking inspiration from retail marketing practices is a good idea as well. In the 1990s the San Jose Public Library established a Marketplace section of the library, in which the new and popular books and DVDs were on shelves right at the entrance where every library patron would pass them. The eye-catching covers of the materials, already marketed by their publishers or studios, did the work of attracting people to pick them up. All the library had to do was place those covers front and center to put them into the hands of their patrons (Molaro & White, 2015). The perk of utilizing a retail model is that it's like a shortcut. In SJPL's case, it did not have to spend time finding ways to market its materials, but rather simply found a way to market the library itself more effectively.

Don't reinvent the wheel when it comes to technology help; simply take inspiration from big box stores or other similar services. In both cases, the library can take advantage of the existing familiarity that consumers have with those stores to minimize the amount of learning library patrons have to do when the space or staffing model changes.

Informal Marketing

Part of the risk and inherent challenge of starting a specialized team is shrinking the potential audience of people your staff can help. A generalist can help almost anyone in the library. Once you specialize staff, you narrow the focus to a smaller group. As a result, the service needs to be marketed both formally and informally. Much of the informal marketing comes from the space design discussed previously in this chapter. With technology desks being in line of sight to the front desks and front doors of the library, they are easily discovered. With the help of handoffs from generalist staff, the technology specialist staff become known to patrons.

In some ways, informal marketing is attracting the eye. Arapahoe Libraries strategically placed a 3D printer near the tech desks, where tech specialists taught people about 3D design and 3D printing when their eyes were drawn to it. Think of a bakery, where one can see all of the tasty options available front and center in a display case (Mathews & Soistmann, 2016). When the library merchandizes 3D prints and its gadgets, library patrons are more likely to discover and be tempted to check out these materials or try out the service. Arapahoe Libraries used this technique to let patrons know about the tech troubleshooting services the tech specialist team could offer. The tech specialist team also experimented with Raspberry Pi, displaying slide-shows on nearby projectors. These have the dual benefit of being an eye-catching display and a geeky technology the team can talk to people about.

Technology specialists in Arapahoe Libraries offer technology demos, anything from a Photoshop demonstration to an overview of the coding tool Treehouse. These also allowed for some informal marketing and showed patrons the type of questions they could come to the tech desk to ask. Patrons are not necessarily asking for one-on-one appointments to learn Arduino, so the tech team take it upon themselves to show patrons this is a resource that the library has and can teach.

Formal Marketing

Formal marketing for tech services does not look much different from any other marketing for your library. Flyers, newsletters, word of mouth, and social media advertising are all viable options. Remember that when working on flyers and any promotional material, you want to promote both the service and the information on them. Do not make a flyer that says "technology help now available!" without including ways to book an appointment or find the whens and hows of the service. Try advertising new digital services along with classes on how to use them (Tanzi, 2016). Similar thinking applies to technology help services. Promote both the service and how to easily get help from it.

Giveaways are another way to think outside the box when marketing tech services (Bizzle & Flora, 2015). Rather than a bookmark or pen, a giveaway like a flash drive or a branded stylus for a tablet can be a great way to make the connection to technology services. Unexpected or exciting perks like these can help spread word-of-mouth marketing for your library. Whenever a technology specialist gives away a 3D print, there's a chance the recipient will show a friend and say, "Hey, look at this cool thing I got at the library!" The unique physical object a patron goes home with is a reminder of that service that the library offers. Many marketing experts emphasize that library staff need to be brand ambassadors. They are the ones interacting with the customers, so they need to be empowered to make small special moments like these happen to create advocates out of their customers (Watson-Lakamp, 2015).

Another technological innovation to keep in mind with in-library marketing is digital signage. These setups can be as simple as an LCD television with a computer hooked up to it running a PowerPoint presentation. They allow you to create a paperless, highly customizable marketing tool that can catch the eye just as well as or better than traditional signage. A bonus of having this at or near a technology desk would be to find a dual use purpose for it: as a second screen for mirroring the tech specialist's laptop for demonstrations or classes and as a marketing display the rest of the time.

As advised in the community analysis section, make an effort to market outside of your library walls. Patrons may not expect in-depth, expert technology help in their public library. And why would they? It has never been formally offered in many libraries. This is why a specific marketing effort is crucial to the successful launch of a tech specialist service. Otherwise, library patrons and the community alike will continue using the library in the same way and expecting the same services they always have. An Arapahoe Libraries staff member came across a tech column in the newspaper in which a reader asked about a service that could help her troubleshoot her iPad. This person did not want to just take it to the Apple Store and get it fixed; she was looking for someone who could sit down with her and really teach her the steps. The columnist recommended a myriad of local paid services, but neglected to mention the public library. Of course, the staff member made the effort to reach out to the journalist to let her know about the library! This serves as a reminder that many people simply assume they need to pay for services like these, and a focused marketing effort is really needed to correct those expectations.

Marketing the Experience

Your marketing effort should focus not on the technology help itself, but on the end result, the experience your library patrons can have. Market the fact that your techs can help load e-books on personal devices; market one-on-one sessions with a tech specialist to learn to build one's own Web site. These end results are more tangible than marketing "technology assistance." People need to be specifically told what type of help they can get; do not make assumptions when it comes to marketing your services. Much as Apple's former CEO said regarding the Apple Store's success, the experience is more important than the product.

Personalization is a great way to market the experience over the product. Putting a face on technology help is meaningful, as it takes away the hesitation a library patron might feel when trying a new service or approaching a staff member she or he does not know. A huge inspiration is Multnomah

County Library's My Librarian program. It is a reader's advisory initiative that truly puts a face on each of its librarians. Library patrons can videoconference, set up appointments, and send in forms to receive personalized materials recommendations from their librarian of choice. Professional photographs and reading tastes for each librarian are included on the Web site and give the user the taste-matching type of information one might see on a dating Web site, to help select a librarian (for taste in books, not date-ability, of course) (Kastner, 2015).

Services like this beg the question: Why not take this personalized approach and adapt it to technology help in the library? Put the technology specialist's face out there, including her or his interests and specialties, both tech- and non-tech-related. Although one should encourage each tech specialist to be interchangeable in terms of knowledge and skills, finding a tech specialist who designed her own Web site or a tech specialist who loves to cosplay might push the library patron to book an appointment with that particular staff member or inspire an idea for a project to learn together.

Another consideration along the same lines to market the tech specialists in the community is embedded librarianship. Embedding a librarian usually involves spending time in an institution or activity outside the public library, such as in a local public school. Networking and going outside the library walls can create connections in the community and foster more word-of-mouth communication about library services (Lucas-Alfieri, 2015). Similarly, embedding a tech specialist at a local makerspace, retirement home, school, or other nonprofit would be a fantastic way to market the service and extend its reach.

AFFORDABLE ALTERNATIVES

Space design can have a wide spectrum of price ranges and options. Early iterations of the technology desks at Arapahoe Libraries were spare rolling laptop desks that were used to test out the viability and visibility of certain areas. To this day, the best desks are fairly affordable standing desks from IKEA. This is an area in which libraries can hire architects and interior designers or simply do it on their own, depending on budget. These experts seem to love suggesting pricy, custom options, but keep in mind there is a lot of room for savings and creativity. Need to paint a wall to draw the eye or separate out an area? Gather together some volunteers or staff to paint it on a national holiday or while the library is closed. Moving furniture and rearranging rooms can also be simple with a crew of willing helpers, rewarded with hot slices of pizza upon completion. Make beautiful custom signage by partnering with a nearby makerspace for help or reach out to local artists. You can negotiate for the use of free art in return for a semipermanent public location and curation.

Marketing does not need to be overly expensive. Establish positive relationships with the local newspaper or magazine and receive free or reduced price ad space each month to promote programs. A recent conference speaker, a marketing department head, stapled fun-size candy bars to flyers to add a little value and excitement to the promotional piece. Word-of-mouth marketing is free of charge. As mentioned for embedded librarianship, consider sending a staff member to a nonlibrary book club, a local makerspace, the rotary club, or any other outside organization to be a library advocate and representative outside your walls. Digital signage is definitely a place for potential savings, as such signs cut out printer costs and worries about the "evergreen" nature of the materials you are putting out.

Teaching Technology

If you have been following the book's process step by step, you have now arguably reached the most important section of the book, technology training and education. You now have tech staff and a lovely space for them to provide great tech help; how can you make sure you are doing a great job of teaching library patrons who come through the doors for help? How can you make sure you are teaching, not just fixing, a library patron's technology problems? After all, traditional library philosophy is all about equal access and informal learning, and you now have a great opportunity to put both into practice.

HOW ADULTS LEARN

It can be challenging to teach and explain technology in a way that works for the average learner. There are different learning styles: visual, auditory, and kinesthetic (by feel). Some might prefer to learn how to use an iPad by simply fiddling (kinesthetic), some might hope to listen to instructions on it (auditory), and yet others might prefer to watch a demonstration (visual). In a classroom environment with multiple learners, it can be challenging to accommodate all learning styles, but making an effort to cover the bases can guarantee a higher level of understanding. Here's an example of how to teach to all learning styles. Open a Word document. For auditory learners, explain where to find the start button, programs, and Office folder. For visual learners, perform the actions on your computer while your students watch. For kinesthetic learners, ask them to follow along on their own computers.

It is also important to take into consideration the age of the adults you are working with. There are three general groups of adults: early, middle, and late. Early adults are most likely career oriented, so immediately usable skills are the ideal outcome of a class for them. Late adults may have a harder time with curriculum, so a slower paced class that encourages talking with fellow classmates is best. Consider this story about an older student who repeatedly came to an e-mail basics course. Over time, the instructor eventually discovered that the student was learning little by little and enjoyed the socialization during the classes (Farmer, 2011). Middle adults are somewhere in between and likely in a late career stage, so they may be interested in both new skills that will benefit their careers and the collaborative social learning of an older adult class.

When considering age, also consider the level of what you are teaching. A big challenge in teaching adults is finding a balance in exercises that engage the learner but do not overwhelm her or him (West, 2011). Learners do want to be challenged, but they don't want to be discouraged. Similarly, by necessity, basics classes must be taught on a spectrum between very basic and advanced, which has the danger of satisfying nobody (West, 2011). That said, it's better to remain at this point on the spectrum than to teach to the lowest level attendees.

People learn best when they have a stake in what they are learning (Houghton-Jan, 2010). In a computer class, the instructor might first explain why Facebook can be a useful and even necessary tool in someone's life before jumping into the material; context is key. Just showing the clicks necessary to perform a function does not mean students will remember them. Explain what knowledge the class attendees will leave with. This philosophy can play well with the theory of constructivist learning, which theorizes that learners draw from life experience and make connections to concepts from those experiences (Gerding, 2007). Commonly utilized tools that could be considered constructivist are analogies and metaphors. These can take abstract technological concepts and bring them into a more digestible format. During a class or a one-on-one session, a technology trainer might explain a search engine like Google as being similar to the yellow pages of the phonebook or compare an SD card in a camera to a modern film canister. Technologically averse learners can get caught up in jargon, and the use of analogies can help bring the focus back to clear concepts. To make the best use of analogies and their role in constructivist learning, however, you must be sure to use analogies that are familiar to learners. For example, an analogy about the yellow pages may confuse a millennial.

Adults especially have ample life experience, so capitalizing on that existing knowledge is a great way to tap into a higher learning potential for that population (Farmer, 2011). Perhaps a baby boomer recognizes similarities between functions on a typewriter she used in the past and functions in Microsoft Word, which produces an ah-ha moment. Keep in mind, though, that experiential learning can have negative impacts as well. If, for example, the learner had negative past experiences regarding technology, tapping into those experiences would likely create an unpleasant learning environment (Farmer, 2011). That's why it's important to check in with learners periodically, to see how they are responding to your content.

In any instruction, whether formal or informal, tech staff need to define their terms. This does not necessarily mean they should act like a dictionary and spout out definitions. But, for example, many people do not know what *browser* means. So instead of just saying "open your Internet browser," you might instead say "open your Internet browser. It's called Firefox, it's the circular blue and orange icon on the left side of your screen." Doing these checks on yourself is crucial. West (2011) points out that library jargon we in the field often use, like *reader's advisory*, *database*, and *OPAC*, is met with confusion outside of the library world, so be sure to have the same consideration for those who are not conversant in the tech world.

TYPES OF TECH TRAINING

Library staff can provide technology training and assistance to patrons in a variety of ways. Different formats, as described in the following sections, better suit different audiences. Also keep in mind that topics and spaces and some formats are more time and resource intensive than others. Although frequent one-on-one sessions for one particular patron might net you good will from that individual, this is obviously not the best utilization of time to serve your entire community.

Self-Guided Training

Self-guided tech training offers a huge benefit to both your staff and patrons. It can be as simple as pointing a patron to an online resource that has the needed information or it can be performed with library staff–generated handouts. Another benefit of self-guided learning is that adults learn best in an environment in which they may choose the topic and pacing of their learning (Gerding, 2007). Staff-written training resources are great, as they are likely to reflect the most common questions and issues that your library patrons might need help with. Handout topics can be anything from using the copier to downloading music to commonly used HTML tags. These have potential for applications all over the library. In a makerspace, you can provide self-guided project cards that will walk people through a project step by step. People can use these cards to work through a project on their own, give it their own creative spin, and learn some new skills along the way. In a computer lab, a handout can help explain a common issue like attaching files to an e-mail or filetype conversion. Library patrons are sometimes confused about or unfamiliar with the concept and tools in a makerspace, so these project cards are a fantastic way to foster engagement. See appendix C for a sample project card.

A word of warning: although these handouts can be a great way for patrons to empower themselves and learn at their own pace, they should not replace the friendly and personalized assistance staff can give. It is up to staff discretion if a one-on-one appointment, on-the-fly help, or self-guided learning is most appropriate in the moment. It is not good customer service to hand a frustrated patron instructions on troubleshooting a problem without offering any other guidance.

When developing self-guided tech handouts, be sure you or your staff are utilizing resources that have been vetted for quality and accuracy. To make effective handouts, assume the handout will be used independently of any instruction. This means that content needs to be absolutely unambiguous in both content and language. Screenshots with arrows and circles are a much appreciated extra step. In the same vein, do not make any assumptions about the knowledge that the end user possesses. If your handout requires downloading an image from Google, you need to explain the process of opening a browser, putting in search terms, right clicking, saving, et cetera. Consider using bullet points, bolded text, and font size to highlight key points. Be sure to also include white space in handouts to allow for note taking and to improve overall readability. To be inclusive of the widest audience, Gerding (2007) suggests creating different versions of the same exercise geared toward differing comfort levels. In a similar manner, Arapahoe Libraries' coding camp handouts included bonus challenges at the end that tested the knowledge gained during that lesson. These challenges could be skipped by attendees who worked through the content more slowly and could add extra difficulty for those who were learning quickly.

On-the-Fly Training

Often in a public library, you will be doing technology training on the fly. A patron might be using a public computer and wonder why her or his job application isn't submitting, or someone may walk up to a service point with a new tablet and want to know how to access e-books, or someone else will want to know how to scale a model for 3D printing. Interactions like this exemplify why many libraries have chosen to have technology specialist staff on hand, as many of these interactions can be too complex or time-consuming for generalist staff to handle. There are several strategies you can use to ensure these interactions will be as successful as possible, with the patron having accomplished what she or he hoped to and having learned a new skill or new information in the process that can be put to use in the future.

The golden rule of these interactions and technology training in general is to teach, don't touch. You want to take on the role of teacher or guide as opposed to assistant. The patron should always be in the driver's seat, controlling what is happening on whatever device she or he is using. The role of library staff is not to sit down and fill out a job application for a patron, but to guide and encourage that person as she or he learns the necessary skills to complete it. This requires a delicate balance that absolutely has to be reached and is something that all technology specialists need to be on the same page with. If one staff member bends or breaks, it causes a cascading effect of differing expectations from your patrons.

It is important to set boundaries and manage expectations from the start. In most cases, you aren't going to be able to sit down and spend an hour teaching someone how to use the Internet or design a 3D model. Before you begin, let the patron know what you can and cannot do for her or him. At the CTC, staff generally limit on-the-fly interactions to five to ten minutes and are sure to make that clear to the patron from the get go. There are a few benefits to putting a time limit on these interactions. One is to ensure that a single patron isn't monopolizing your time while there are others in need of help. It also encourages the patron to explore and try to do things on her or his own. Often it seems that if there is a staff member standing next to them, people become paralyzed, fearful of doing anything at all without getting input from staff first ("Where do I click now?"). This is likely due to fear of embarrassing themselves by doing something wrong in front of an "expert" or being blamed if something goes wrong. One of the best things you can do for someone learning something new is to help that person overcome the fear of doing something wrong or breaking something. Give people the opportunity to explore on their own (and maybe even click on the wrong thing once or twice to see that the world doesn't end!) and figure out how to fix their own mistakes.

When you have limited time to help someone, sometimes it's more important for that person to "get it" in that moment than it is to explain something perfectly and accurately. Let's say that your patron continually calls the USB port on her computer the URL port, which is not accurate, but she understands what it is and what it does. When teaching technology, you may need to pick and choose what information is most important to teach or correct. Although there is potential for confusion between what "USB" and "URL" stand for in the future, it is more important to take into account what the library patron has capacity for and instead reserve that capacity to teach a concept rather than jargon. You will need to adapt your language, teaching style, and approach based on the skill level of the patron you are helping. It might make sense to show one patron how to use cloud-based document sharing like Google Drive, while it may be better to show another patron how to use physical storage like a flash drive to save her or his work for another time. The end result is the same—the document has been saved—but the concept and teaching are different for each medium. Good technology trainers can discover the skill and comfort levels of the library patron they are working with and alter the approach as they go based on these cues. They have multiple ways to get the same job done for these types of situations.

To ensure successful on-the-fly interactions, start by asking patrons what they are trying to do before you start trying to help. You may be able to show them easier or more effective ways to achieve their goals rather than the methods they are having trouble with. This is essentially your classic reference interview; you may start trying to help update a patron's iPad when she or he was simply asking what the little red number notification on the settings icon meant. Asking questions to clarify what the issue is and what the patron wants to know is absolutely necessary before anything else happens. When you do start troubleshooting or teaching, always explain why you are having patrons do something; this will help them figure things out and troubleshoot on their own in the future. Do not just say "tap on settings"; explain that the settings icon is where you can change volume or brightness and find the latest update version.

During these interactions, be positive and encouraging. One tip is to be sure to blame any issues on the computer or the Web site, not on user error. People can be sensitive about their technology skills or lack thereof, so it is of utmost importance to maintain a friendly demeanor. Also, do not show any signs of impatience like tapping your foot, looking at the clock, or other negative body language. One of the most common compliments about the technology specialist teams at Denver Public Library and Arapahoe Libraries is patience. This is an absolute necessity while teaching technology, and it helps to maximize comfort and foster a good learning environment.

Do not be afraid to not know the answer to the problem immediately. Yes, technology specialists are seen as the technology experts, but pretending to know what the issue is does not help anyone. Being humble and admitting this is a problem you are not familiar with helps the patron feel that her or his question is not "dumb." In these cases, work with the patron to figure out the problem together and tell her or him that is the plan. This is one of the most valuable skills you can teach.

Drop-in Times

Drop-in times are a timeframe you advertise during which people can come in and get technology help. They are not formal or structured classes, more like times when people can stop by and get answers to whatever related questions they have. Drop-in times can cover a specific topic like "e-book help" or "job search open lab" or be more general like "tech Tuesday" or even just "open lab." These unstructured times help catch any errant questions or concerns that your community may have; they can also be great avenues for feedback and a gauge for potential future structured classes if a single topic or question comes up consistently.

To create successful drop-in sessions, try to hold them in a consistent location at a consistent time. When people arrive, have them write down two to three questions they want answered on a piece of paper. This helps them focus on what they really need and can help the tech trainer manage a larger crowd (and reassure them that they will get their questions answered). It also has the added benefit of allowing the tech trainer to gauge the room. If you discover that people have similar questions or devices or skill levels, you can group them together. They can help each other, and chances are they will also be interested in the answers to each other's questions. One potential issue to keep in mind with drop-in times is having more people show up than you expected. If possible, have an extra technology specialist on hand during this time to help with this situation or simply triage and group people as best you can. Make sure to temper patron expectations when it comes to drop-in times, as by definition they are informal and on the spot, so spending 20 minutes on one particular issue for one patron may not be reasonable. More often than not if this is the situation, you have good reason to believe that a program or class might be best suited to a particular subject rather than a drop-in time due to the subject's popularity.

Demos and Tech Petting Zoos

The purpose of a demo or tech petting zoo is to expose people to technology they may not be familiar with. It isn't meant to be an in-depth instructional session, just a quick "check out this cool thing" moment for patrons with a "here's what to do if you want to learn more" component afterward. For instance, you may have a 3D printer sitting on your circulation desk where any patron can see it in action printing an object. Or you may have a table at the front of the library with a staff member demonstrating a variety of tablets, showing off various library resources or cool apps. This can be a great way to have your technology specialist staff proactively connect patrons with technology, rather than sitting back and waiting for tech troubleshooting questions to come to them. Visual excitement really helps to bring people to your demo. One way to do this is to mirror your computer's screen on an external outward-facing monitor to demonstrate visually exciting software like Photoshop or Tinkercad. Demos are also great for outreach events, helping to attract people to your table to chat about cool technology in the library.

Successful demos are usually done on a very relaxed timetable; people should be able to show up anytime and see the tech in action. If you choose a specific time period, be sure to make it clear that the demo can happen any time within that window of time. It should only take a few minutes to explain whatever is being demonstrated, so be sure to have an elevator speech (a brief and well-thought-out explanation of what you will be demonstrating, with a few key bullet points and tips) ready. Check tech blogs and Web sites quickly to see if there's any news on 3D printing, tablets, or whatever specific technology you are demonstrating to encourage discussion. A major rule of thumb is that people should be able to touch and play with whatever you are demonstrating. Drones proved to be problematic with this philosophy, as the library did not feel confident placing the remote control in the hands of a library patron, but the fun of the device and the demo form the interactive component of flying it. If this is the case at your library, but you would still like to demonstrate devices like drones, consider utilizing a liability waiver (a good example can be found at Denver Public Library, https://www.denverlibrary.org/techwaiver). Just how conservative the waiver needs to be tends to vary quite a bit from library to library, but err on the side of placing some trust in your patrons so as to avoid erecting too many obstacles to what you're actually there for: connecting people with technology. With demos, a takeaway is always a bonus. Try 3D printing small flat trinkets like a Green Lantern symbol or the silhouette of a *Dr. Who* TARDIS for outreach events and programs. As mentioned in chapter 4, flash drives or other tech-related giveaways are a good bonus.

Meet-ups

A tech meet-up is an informal gathering of people who are all interested in the same tech topic. Topics can be general, like "Learn to Code," or more specific, like "WordPress Developers." They usually aren't structured, often operating more like study groups or conversations. Content at a given meet-up adapts to the needs of whoever shows up. With tech meet-ups, ideally you want to let the community run the show; the role of the library is really just to provide a space for these like-minded community members to get together and talk, share, or work on projects that interest them. A big benefit of meet-ups is that they bring tech aficionados to you and establish your library as a tech hub in the community with a very low impact on staff.

Successful meet-ups should ideally be facilitated by community members, not library staff. If you are starting a new meet-up, you might have the library host prepare a brief related activity to get the ball rolling, then adjust course to allow the meet-up to run itself over time. A meet-up is a great place to get a feel for what that part of your community needs, so be sure to listen and suggest library resources as appropriate. Have a space available for meet-ups that is aesthetically pleasing and outfitted with plenty of power and data. If Meetup.com is popular in your area, be sure to post your events there! If

Meetup.com is not popular in your area, Craigslist, NextDoor, or any other online community resource that seems popular in your area is your best bet.

Appointments

Scheduled technology help appointments can be a good option for people who need more in-depth help or attention than can be provided when they walk in the door or attend a class. Appointments can also be a good option for people who don't feel comfortable with self-guided learning or group instruction. Or they may simply learn better one on one. Thirty minutes to one hour is generally a good length for an appointment; you can usually get someone to the point of being ready to move forward on her or his own in that timeframe, regardless of the topic. Appointments are very time intensive; you are spending a long time helping just one library patron. That said, appointments can provide a lot of value to the patron and tend to result in effusive patron comments.

One of the best ways to ensure a successful appointment, whether you're working with someone who is getting her or his first e-mail account or someone who is building a Web site, is to ask the patron a lot of questions when you initially set up:

- What do you want to learn, and why?
- Will you be bringing your own device? What kind? What operating system?
- What do you already know? How comfortable are you with computers?

That last question can trip people up sometimes, and guiding them with yes or no questions can help you get the information you need. You can ask if the patron has an e-mail address or has used the software before.

Be sure that the patron has a specific goal for the appointment. "I want to learn how to use a computer" is not a good appointment topic; this is the type of appointment that could last hours, so you might direct a person with this goal to a class at the library or elsewhere. "I want to learn how to post photos on Facebook from my phone" is much better. Set clear boundaries and expectations at the beginning of the appointment and confirm that you understand what the patron is looking for. Say things like "In this appointment, you said you wanted to learn how to X and X, is that right?" and "We have X amount of time to work together. I will be guiding and helping you, but you will be in control."

Classes and Programs

Classes and programs provide a structured time to cover a particular topic, which is a good approach for reaching many people at once, maximizing the staff time you are investing, and for delving deep into particular topics. They can be one-offs, multiple part series, or more intensive programs lasting many weeks, depending on the topic. A one-off class could be best to show-case a single piece of software or a single concept to learn, like "Introduction to Tinkercad" or "Make a Beat in FL Studio." On the other hand, coding tends to lend itself to the intensive series. Coding concepts build upon them-selves much like mathematics, and it can be very challenging to teach any-thing meaningful in a one-off coding class. As a result, coding camps or regular weekly series seem to have the most benefit, but of course they also have the highest impact on staff time. After-school programs could be more intensive, lasting many weeks, and are a great option for teaching technol-ogy in your community. Programs like these tend to grow over time for the social aspect, as the staff and patrons who regularly show up get to know one another. Establishing this authority and trust of knowing one another is especially valuable in after-school programs. They are similarly staff inten-sive but provide amazing education and a value for your community's kids. The rule of thumb with after-school programs is to have a balanced amount of time for unstructured learning and fun. These kids just got out of school; they do not want more school in the library.

CLASS DESIGN

Once you have chosen a topic, it's time to figure out exactly what you're going to teach and how you're going to teach it. The CTC at Denver Public Library uses a process it calls iterative lesson design to create all of its tech programs. Iterative lesson design has several steps, many of which repeat continuously throughout the life of the class: play, write, edit, teach, evaluate.

The first step, play, involves researching and exploring whatever technol-ogy you're going to be teaching. There is a good chance you can find videos or other materials aimed at teaching people how to use a specific technology, so you probably won't have to start from scratch. Play with the software or hardware itself, trying to approach it as someone who has never used it be-fore. Complete a simple project, documenting the steps it takes and paying close attention to what was difficult, unexpected, or unintuitive about the process. Use that experience to build your plan. A sample lesson plan can be found at https://www.denverlibrary.org/ctc/viruses-malware-101.

Now that you are intimately familiar with the technology you want to teach, it's time to come up with a plan and put it in writing. Before you start writing your lesson plan, you need to define your audience. Whom is this class for? What do you think they hope to get out of this workshop? What general skill level are these learners likely to have? You want to tie your content to your audience's interests and experiences as much as possible. This is the first part of the process you'll want to edit. Read through your lesson plan and get a coworker to try the steps for the first edit.

The first thing to decide is what the learning objectives for your class will be. Learning objectives are three to five goals you have for your learners: What should they know, understand, or be able to do once the class is over? All of your content and activities should support these learning objectives. Here are some examples of learning objectives for tech training on varying topics. At the end of this class, students will be able to:

- conduct a search with Google's search engine,
- create strong passwords,
- compose a beat and melody,
- identify signs a computer may be infected with malicious software.

Everything that happens in your class or workshop should support your learning objectives. If an explanation or activity does not support your objectives, it probably belongs in another class. Keeping your objectives in mind can also help prevent you from trying to cover too much material in a class. Covering too much will leave your students feeling overwhelmed.

Now you're ready to teach. The order in which you cover your content is crucial for your students' understanding and retention. Be sure to structure your class so each section builds on and reinforces previously taught skills. Break up your material to keep learners' attention and present materials in a variety of ways. As mentioned previously, using multiple media and methods for different types of learners helps ensure that you are finding the best learning style or preference for each learner. You can switch from lecturing and demonstrating to watching a video to having the students complete a task on their own. Spend 10 minutes explaining what copy and paste is and why someone might use it. Then show a short video tutorial, then demonstrate to the students.

You want your students to have an organic user experience and learn as they go. Constructivist learning concepts can be well exercised here if you build your class around completing a project or task, ideally a project that is likely to be relevant to your students' past experience or daily lives. Instead of teaching copy and paste, font formatting, and line spacing, teach students how to create a flyer for a lost dog and cover each of those skills as it comes up in that context. With this method, instead of trying to memorize a series of clicks and menus, the students see the real-world purpose of each skill and how the skills all fit together.

Before you teach your class in a classroom, try to get feedback on your plan from at least two other people. Talk to people with different levels of experience to review your plan. A person who is new to the topic and an "expert" will notice different things and be able to provide different types of useful feedback. You can ask coworkers, volunteers, friends, or even library patrons for feedback. Remember that everything in your plan should support your learning objectives. Once you have started offering your class to the public, there are several ways you can evaluate how successful it is (or isn't). We delve into these in detail in the next chapter. Once you have started teaching your class to the public, you will repeat the process of playing, writing, editing, teaching, and evaluating forever. Here's where you want to implement the iterative approach and use this feedback and your own experience to edit, edit, edit. A good class is never "done."

COMMON CHALLENGES AND SOLUTIONS

Following are recommendations to help solve common challenges of teaching technology in all formats.

- **Technology doesn't work the way it should.** At some point, something will not work the way you want it to. The screen won't display properly, a Web site will have changed its layout the night before, or you'll get search results you weren't expecting. The possibilities of things that can go wrong are endless when you are working with technology. But don't worry! This isn't a problem; it's an opportunity that can be a great learning experience for your students. When something goes wrong in the middle of a training session, remain calm and go through the process you normally would to troubleshoot the problem, but narrate each step for your students. For example, if the screen goes blank while you are teaching, say something like, "Okay, let's make sure the power cord is plugged in, now let's check and see that the VGA/HDMI cord is tightly plugged into the monitor so the computer can communicate with the screen" and so forth. This process teaches your students that technology problems happen for everyone, even the experts, and they're not the end of the world. It also teaches them the correct vocabulary to describe the tech problem that is being experienced. Finally, they get to experience how a real-world tech problem that they themselves might encounter is solved.

- **Someone asks a question, and you don't know the answer.** Much like experiencing a tech problem while teaching, fielding a question you can't answer is more of an opportunity than a problem. As with any other reference question, the best response is something in the vein of "That's a great question! I don't know the answer, but let's figure it out!" Now you have the opportunity to show your students how to find the answers they are looking for. As with the tech problem scenario, narrate every step you take to find the answer so they can learn how to do it themselves. Show students how to effectively use a search engine or a help menu to find information, tutorials, videos, and forums that can answer their questions. Model good search strategies and talk about how you choose which site to visit based on the results. ("Since this is a Microsoft product, the official Microsoft site is probably going to have good information. I can tell this is the Microsoft Web site by the URL.") Explain that if you have a question about technology, chances are that someone else has had the same question before, and the answer is likely available in one medium or another online. This skill is more important than anything else you'll teach, because once learners understand how to find answers they are empowered to solve problems on their own. It is also good for students to see that you, the great technology teaching expert, do not know everything there is to know, and it's no big deal. Let your students know that the answers are out there and accessible to anyone once you know how to find them.

- **Students have varying skill levels or the wrong skill level for the topic.** It is common to have students with varying skill levels in your program, and it can be a challenge to teach them simultaneously. One of the best ways to address this is by setting clear expectations at the beginning of class. Write the topics you are going to cover on a whiteboard or display them on your screen to give students a better understanding of what will be covered in the class. Let them know you will not be able to cover topics outside the scope of the class, but you can tell them about additional resources at the end of class. Also tell students before you get started what skills they will need to participate successfully in the class. Let them know that they are welcome to stay and observe even if they cannot keep up, but you cannot provide individual help with required skills. For example, part of an instructor's introduction for an Internet class might sound something like this: "If you aren't comfortable using a mouse yet you are probably going to have a hard time keeping up in this class. You are welcome to stay and absorb as much as you can, but I will not be able to give you individual help because that is beyond the scope of this class. I would be happy to talk to anyone after class about resources for learning mouse skills."

- **Students may know more than you do on a topic.** Occasionally you get a student who knows more about the subject than you do (or at least thinks she or he does). The student may interrupt to tell you that you are doing it wrong or to add unnecessary detail or off-topic information. Highly knowledgeable students can actually become your allies in the classroom, helping other students keep up or providing relevant personal examples. The trick is to let them participate without dominating the class. Try to validate their knowledge and experience while also reinforcing your role as the instructor. Say something like: "You're right, that's a good point, and it's clear that you have a lot of experience on this subject, but since we have limited time today we aren't going to be able to cover all the details. We can talk more about it after class if anyone is interested."

AFFORDABLE ALTERNATIVES

Depending on how robust your staffing levels are, how many methods you can use to teach technology will vary. If your staff need to cover the desk most of the time, perhaps having lots of one-on-one appointments and classes is unrealistic. The CTC at the Denver Public Library helps alleviate this problem by using volunteers to help teach classes and the more basic one-on-one appointments. Drop-in times are a good way to maximize your staff time, especially with our recommended method of grouping people with similar needs. If you are having a hard time justifying taking staff off the floor to teach a class or program, think of it like this: Is it more time efficient to help five patrons five different times to learn how to attach a document to an e-mail, or is it more efficient to teach five to ten patrons how to accomplish that task in a class?

There's also room for cost savings if you and your staff write great class plans. Great class plans should allow nearly any instructor, volunteer or not, to teach a successful class. This means that if your only staff member conversant in Photoshop gets another job, you still have that person's knowledge in the form of the class, and you can continue teaching that class with another instructor. It also makes utilizing volunteers to teach classes much easier. You can trust your staff to veer a little from the content, but you want volunteers to stick to the material, at least at first. If you do not have the time or resources to develop your own materials from scratch, there are tons of resources out there that you can use or tweak. Check out the following resources:

- denverlibrary.org/ctc-classes
- http://www.nypl.org/tech-connect
- digitallearn.org
- gcflearnfree.org

Your location is also important, though some libraries may not have the luxury of a computer lab or classroom to teach in. As an alternative, see if there is a school or community center in the area that has a computer lab or classroom you could utilize. Depending on the setup of your library, you may be able to reserve and make use of some of your public computers. If your library has any laptops, use them in a meeting room. If you have more learners than laptops, partner up. If you need cheap computers, Chromebooks can be purchased for around $200. Laptops are limited in some capacities, but for any sort of Internet, browser, or mousing class, they can work great. If you can't access any sort of learner computers, have learners follow along while the instructor demonstrates with one computer and a projector. Be sure to provide handouts and room for taking notes.

6

Evaluating Tech Services

- Why Evaluate?
- Setting Targets
- Picking Your Metrics
- Collecting Data from Patrons
- Program and Class Evaluation
- Staff Evaluation
- Community Impacts
- Affordable Alternatives

WHY EVALUATE?

The key to success for any library service, especially a newly implemented one, is evaluation. This chapter provides advice on how to evaluate the data you have collected to be sure you are continually improving. All aspects of technology services connected to evaluation: results from your community needs analysis, staff, the effectiveness with which you teach, and a host of others. The evaluation process should begin before you ever offer a service or program. The process should tie in closely with your community's needs and strategic plan. Be sure to tie the evaluation process closely to the community needs and data analyses from chapter 2.

Most libraries are required to keep certain data for the Public Libraries Survey, a standardized survey the Institute of Museum and Library Services provides (IMLS, 2014). While these data are useful to provide a standard against which to compare other libraries, they should not be the only data you collect for your library. There will always come a time when you will need to justify your actions or expenditures, and the Public Libraries Survey may not necessarily provide all of the specific data you need to do so. Since libraries are for the benefit of the public and most often funded by the public, it is especially important for them to keep track of the effectiveness of their services. Although public opinion of libraries is generally high, libraries need to be good stewards of their public funding and formally prove their value in their communities. As public servants, surely libraries also want to know if they are effectively serving their communities to be able to improve upon what they are doing. This is especially important when it comes to technology services, as technology tends to cause change so quickly that an agile and iterative approach is needed.

While many libraries are required by their states to collect basic statistics, few institutions actually shape any sort of strategy or goal around them (Matthews, 2004). If you have been following along in this book, data collection revolving around community needs from chapter 2 should help you ensure that any evaluation is aligned with your strategic plan. Instead of boasting about a 5 percent increase in makerspace attendance from the first year, you can say that you have achieved your strategic plan of increasing STEM interactions in the community and use these data as proof. Data need an explanation and supporting story; you cannot expect even your biggest stakeholders to make these connections themselves.

Data can be incredibly helpful in allocating resources where they are needed. At Arapahoe Libraries, the technology specialists serve six branches with differing needs. Data are used to see where the most questions are, which helps the library decide which location needs a tech specialist every day or every other day. The data help the library decide what the peak hours are and when people are coming in with the most questions. Since the library has established a baseline with question complexity, it has been able to demonstrate an overall increase in question complexity over time with data as well.

An overall trend in data collection in libraries is to establish warm and fuzzy feelings about the library in the community rather than finding efficiencies and ways to boost effectiveness (Matthews, 2004). While it certainly does not hurt to maintain positive feelings about the library among one's users, for the purposes of meaningful data collection, libraries need to be sure that their methods focus on measures of effectiveness. It is easy to get caught up in "feel good" things like early literacy and democratization of resources that libraries do offer to the community, but these things need specificity and measurement to ensure a library is reaching its goals and utilizing public resources to the best of its abilities.

In a study, community leaders and locals ranked measures they felt most represented a library that was utilizing its resources effectively. Some of these measures included the convenience of the library's open hours, the breadth of materials available, and staff's ability to help (Matthews, 2004). Collecting data on these topics rather than focusing on the warm and fuzzy philosophies should help libraries dig down deeper into ways they can legitimately improve rather than get evaluation results that focus on positive, but largely unconstructive, feedback.

SETTING TARGETS

Setting targets to measure success can be difficult, and there is no magic formula. Combine past experience, input from various stakeholders, results from similar (and nonlibrary) organizations, and research to come up with your targets (Matthews, 2004). There can be a lot of overlap with your community needs assessment, so be sure to consult your data and research from that as well. Technology plans or strategic plans should outline goals for the library, so these may very well serve as your potential targets. Another way to see how you measure up is to consult benchmarks. The Bill and Melinda Gates Foundation has implemented the EDGE Assessment as one way to measure. These assessments provide various benchmarks on the topics of tech programs and services, the library's role as a beneficial community institution, and the library's ability to best utilize the resources available to it (EDGE, 2015). If your library does not reach some of these benchmarks, these can be a part of your future strategic plan or goals to reach at a later date.

You can also use your first year of a new service or program to set a baseline and work on improving upon those results. However, it is important to remember capacity and resource limitations when setting targets as well. For instance, you are probably not going to increase tech class attendance by 20 percent every year forever. At a certain point you will run out of space, time, staff, or even people who need a particular type of training. A small branch with 4 staff members will never be able to run as many programs as a large central library with 200 staff members. A capacity index takes all of those things into consideration, compares needs with resources available, and then assigns a value that can help individual locations figure out how many programs they should be able to run. You also need to consider the ideal scenario for effectiveness and providing value to the patron. If you are teaching a class on Internet basics, even if you have 100 seats available, trying to teach 100 students Internet basics is unlikely to be effective.

PICKING YOUR METRICS

When choosing metrics, you are basically asking: What do you want to know, and why? Your targets and benchmarks can help shape these questions. Perhaps one of your benchmarks is to have 10 percent better computer class attendance than a neighboring public library system. Or you may have just launched a new technology help service at the library: How can you make sure it is a success, and how can you ensure it continues to be a success? You may want to know the age of the average patron the staff help, the length of time it takes for a question to be answered, and the complexity of that question. You may want to know the most popular times that questions come in. Break down these different measures when you are deciding what to evaluate. An easy rule of thumb is to run through the basic journalistic method of who, what, where, when, why, and how.

There is a basic framework for these evaluative questions, known as input measures, process measures, output measures, and outcomes (Matthews, 2004). *Input measures* are the resources given to the library; this could be an annual budget, number of staff hours, or number of tech gadgets available. These measures start your analysis with a line of thinking that "this is what we have put in, what have we gotten out" of those resources. Keep in mind, though, that the data must be used in a comparison with other data you collect for the most rounded evaluation (Matthews, 2004).

Process measures are essentially helping to measure the exact resource cost of a service. A common library comparison might be measuring the average length of time it takes to shelve a cart of fiction books. The time it takes multiplied by the staff's hourly salary tells you the approximate resource cost of that process. You could pay a professional lawyer a competitive salary to provide law advice in a public library, but the cost of employing that individual compared to the overall benefit to the community may be too much. A process measure might find that technology interactions on average take double the time of any other type of interaction.

Output measures are probably the most common form of data collected in libraries. They measure how much a particular resource is being used. These could include reference interaction numbers, computer use data, or overall circulation numbers. Outcome measures are the overall impact of a library on its community, the general good that the library is doing for its patrons. Keep in mind that large numbers associated with these measures do not necessarily equate with success; there are many other factors at play. If 200 people show up at an event your library planned, but the event cost $5,000 to put together, could you consider that an overall success? One way to tackle these conundrums is to measure per capita costs or do a cost benefit analysis. Measure the number of attendees compared to the monetary/staffing cost of a program, library visits compared to the size of your local population, and number of technology questions compared to the number of library visits in a day. These help give more context to the output measures (Matthews, 2004).

Output measures of overall community good tend to be correlations and are difficult to measure. One can say something like "libraries tend to raise real estate value in surrounding communities," but it is difficult to draw direct, measurable lines from one to the other ("Minnesota Public Libraries' return on investment," 2011). You can also think of it like this: an individual who uses the coding education resource Treehouse through the library gets a related job shortly afterward. Although this individual may not have gotten the job without using the library's resources, it is impossible to measure that transaction as an overall community impact (Matthews, 2004).

As an example, look at these measures through the lens of the technology specialist service at Arapahoe Libraries. Some of the input measures are an annual staff salary and technology budget to pay technology specialists and to keep them equipped with work technology tools and creative technology tools. The process measures are the competitive hourly wage; technology skills are in high demand in our community, so this wage is a little higher than our generalist floor staff's wage. The overall *outcomes* are difficult to measure, but there are plenty of anecdotes, such as the local Best Buy or Sprint store sends customers with technology issues to the library for the great personalized service. Technology specialists also receive the most positive patron comments of any department; the positive impact can be vaguely gauged, but not in the exacting way that the other measures allow.

Output measures for technology specialists at Arapahoe Libraries are thorough, bordering on obsessive. Technology specialists use a Google form to track every interaction they have, one form for each of the six libraries they serve (see appendix D). This practice was implemented when the service started to establish a baseline. This would give the library something to measure against for future statistics collection. The technology specialist department was allocated a somewhat bare-bones budget, so illustrating effectiveness and demand with these data for future growth opportunities was beneficial as well. Google forms measure duration of the interaction, number of patrons, referral method (walk-up, staff handoff, scheduled program, etc.), category (3D printing, basic computer help, e-resources help, etc.), and complexity.

Complexity is tough to measure, but technology specialists utilize a set of criteria for each number, 0–3. A 0 is the most basic tech question, like connecting one's device to the library's wireless Internet. A 1 is a routine tech question, such as resetting an e-mail password or uploading a smartphone photo to Facebook. A 2 is getting a little tougher, ideally the majority of interactions a technology specialist helps with. These are too lengthy or difficult for generalist staff to handle and may involve some tricky fixes like updating a computer's driver, removing malware, or troubleshooting Adobe IDs as they relate to e-books. A 3 is uncommon and is a truly difficult interaction that stretches tech staff's knowledge past what they possess, such as collaborating with someone developing a game for beta technology like Oculus Rift or getting in depth with reworking source files for makerspace projects on a laser cutter. Measuring complexity is, well, complex, as each technology specialist has a different background and comfort level with varying subjects. To one technology specialist, troubleshooting a 3D printer is a 2, but to another that would be a clear 3. The specific examples above help quite a bit.

A standing meeting agenda item about interaction difficulty can also help ensure output measures are accurate. You might ask staff in the meeting what interactions recently really stretched their knowledge and what questions have become common. Keep in mind that complexity will be an evolving measure as well, as over time the more difficult questions may degrade once staff are comfortable with those interactions. Also notable about measuring complexity is that duration does not necessarily dictate difficulty. A level 1 question may take 45 minutes to answer due to the patron's technology comfort, or a level 3 question may be difficult but take only 10 minutes to work through. See appendix E for a readout of the data Arapahoe Libraries collects on technology specialist interactions.

COLLECTING DATA FROM PATRONS

Thus far you have been collecting data about your library and your interactions for the purposes of improving, but for the purposes of tech improvements, consider collecting data from library patrons themselves. Especially in pursuit of improving your technology services, it can be highly valuable to collect information on their technology skills or interests. New York Public Library's TechConnect has a novel solution in the form of a short and visual survey (see http://techconnect-files.nypl.org/What's%20Your%20Tech%20 Profile%20_NEW/story.html). It asks questions about the level of interest when a new device or technology is released; relationship to e-mail; and other questions that help evaluate whether someone is a tech guru, a beginner, or somewhere in between. On the results page, the survey recommends technology classes that might interest a user at the patron's level of knowledge (New York Public Library/NYPL TechConnect, 2016). A fun and quick survey like this is a great way to both collect valuable data and help advertise the resources available to users.

Other than assessments like the one NYPL uses, consider evaluating the technology skills of your library patrons via surveys, observation, or focus groups. Chapter 2 includes lots of information on surveys and survey bias, so be sure to check there if you are considering utilizing a survey as a tool to measure patron technology competencies. Focus groups are also covered in chapter 2; these could be made up of staff, patrons, or both, depending on the data you are looking to collect. Focus groups traditionally involve interviews or talking points for the group to discuss, with a data collector sitting in to record everything.

Observation is probably the simplest after focus groups and surveys and might involve simply asking your technology staff what they have observed (see the "Program and Class Evaluation" section below for more information on observation as a data collection tool). The Institute of Museum and Library Services (2002) recommends observation for collecting helpful supplemental information to a survey.

PROGRAM AND CLASS EVALUATION

Since programs and classes can involve quite a bit of staff time and preparation, it is important to use metrics to ensure that time is well spent. If your staff spent weeks planning an iMovie course, but only one person showed up, you might want to reconsider the ratio of time spent versus patron benefit. There are many, many factors that can go into an unsuccessful program or class. It could be that the time it was offered was inconvenient, the community near the branch it was offered at has little interest in video editing, or the program description did not make it clear what iMovie can do. There are always multiple factors in play; remember that when using and collecting data you need to paint an entire picture rather than take one factor and write a narrative from there. The data collection that the technology specialists at Arapahoe Libraries use for interactions, outlined above, also works well for programs. It finds out how many patrons came to the program, where it was, the complexity of the interactions, and the subject of the program. Utilizing these data and staff knowledge on locations, time, and attendance, you can make an educated guess about why a class or program was or was not successful.

Observation is another great way to evaluate programs and classes. Observations can be done by other staff regularly throughout the year. Peer observation is preferable to a supervisor or manager observing the class, which may make the instructor act differently or nervously. Peers can provide feedback on the content and flow of the class and the instructor's teaching style. Feedback can be loose and informal; just have the observer chat with the teacher after the program about what went well and what could be improved. You can also create a feedback form or survey for observers to fill out. In either case, it's important that everyone is on the same page as far as what to look for and what kinds of things are likely to make a program successful.

When observing, take into account environment, communication, content, and engagement. Here is what to look for as an observer in each category:

- ENVIRONMENT
  - Sets appropriate expectations.
  - Creates an environment of mutual respect and rapport.
  - Starts class with introductions and explains classroom "rules."
- COMMUNICATION
  - Communicates clearly, effectively, and accurately.
  - Demonstrates flexibility and responsiveness in adjusting instruction to meet student need.
  - Clearly communicates class objectives to students.
- CONTENT
  - Demonstrates knowledge of subject.
  - Covers concepts outlined in lesson plan.

- ○ Has appropriate pacing.
- ○ Explains how students can find help on their own.
- ENGAGEMENT
    - ○ Creates enough opportunities for students to ask questions.
    - ○ Connects students' prior knowledge, life experiences, and interests in the instructional process.
    - ○ Ties information to practical, real-life situations.
    - ○ Checks in with students to determine if they are progressing toward stated objectives.
    - ○ Gives students the opportunity for hands-on practice when appropriate.
    - ○ Summarizes and fits into context what has been taught.

In addition to observation, post-class or post-program surveys are also very popular. Denver Public Library asks questions about the pacing and difficulty of the class, such as the following:

Did you gain a valuable skill that you can use alone?
How was the instructor of the class?

The observation and post-class survey have very similar values, and through this redundancy in data collection the instructor will get well-rounded feedback from both peers and learners. Being able to drill down to the specific instructor and the specific class gets one very valuable information. Maybe a certain class's pace is off, or maybe you have an employee who has a tough time teaching in a lecture format. Much like Arapahoe Libraries' survey that staff fill out after a tech interaction, it is important to capture these data right after the interaction happens.

STAFF EVALUATION

Much as programs and technology interactions need evaluation to grow, technology specialist staff also need evaluation to grow. These evaluations should be conducted regularly and are likely to be easily rolled into whichever performance review measures your organization has in place already. Most staff evaluations tend to have different focus areas, like communication, adaptability, leadership, and so forth. Each focus area is then measured: doesn't meet expectations, meets expectations, or exceeds expectations. The structure of these evaluations allows for a supervisor or manager to document thoughts about what areas an employee is doing well in and what an employee can improve upon. Supervisors should be diligent and thorough in collecting data on their employees via their own observation, peer review, and self-reports from employees. This will provide the most rounded view of a particular employee's performance.

It is ideal if you are able to customize the areas for evaluation rather than use preset criteria for all staff; this results in a review most suited to your specialty. Sections on customer service, adaptability, and professional growth tend to be the most important for tech specialist staff. Sound familiar? These are the same qualities we recommended looking for when hiring staff in chapter 3. Think about this process in two parts: hire for these skills, then use evaluation measures to be sure that your staff retain and grow them.

Technology specialist evaluations tend to focus on expansion and learning. This can be the type of job that causes eventual burnout due to the challenge and volume of questions day to day. Focusing on professional growth helps address this issue and helps the employees discover what new projects or challenges might excite them. If one of your staff is less than excited about the prospect of doing more coding clubs for teenagers, perhaps it is time to shake things up and have her explore a new area of expertise. If your staff member is challenged by a question he has not answered before, his goal should be to brush up on that subject for the next time that subject comes up. If budget allows, finding tech conferences, local meet-ups, or tech trainings can be a great way to help grow staff and excite them about different possibilities in their expertise.

Adaptability is perhaps the most important quality of a technology specialist. It is impossible for anyone to be an expert in all things, so more important than knowing any technology issue that can come up is the ability to adapt to the situation. Inevitably, issues will arise that tech specialists do not know the answer to, and they need to be highly adaptable to such a situation, doing research and trying various techniques on the spot. A technology specialist should be conversant in both Android and iOS, and a technology specialist should be willing to work with any browser or software that comes along. Personal preference is fine, but adaptability is the willingness to work with other platforms or solve problems in other ways when necessary. During evaluation periods, the supervisor should look back on these situations and ensure that her or his staff have been ready to approach these occasionally difficult or uncomfortable situations with a willingness to adapt.

Finally, as with any patron-facing job, customer service skills are tantamount to personal success. With technology specialists, this often equates to having a friendly conversation while waiting for a driver to download or a picture to upload. Technology specialists should be approachable and friendly at their desk on the floor, not too engrossed in a computer. A great customer service interaction should be fruitful, educational, and pleasant for the library patron. Keep in mind that everyone has her or his own style of customer service interactions, so be sure not to give high marks only to your extroverts or the most chatty; your staff with other personality types are just as capable of exhibiting good customer service skills, albeit in their own style.

COMMUNITY IMPACTS

The entire reason you go through the process of data collection is to ensure positive community impact. In one form or another, these are the *outcome* measures in the evaluation model outlined above. They should represent differences, things that have changed for the better since you implemented a particular strategy or service. The American Library Association recommends using the SMART method to measure outcomes. S stands for specific, meaning these outcomes should be strategic. Dig down to exactly what outcomes you want, avoiding broad measures at all costs. The M means measurable, meaning your outcomes should not be stories or anecdotes, but measurable data. Be sure to use benchmarks or per capita comparisons to give context to these measurements. Your outcomes should be attainable (A), within scope and preferably in line with your strategic plan. The outcomes should also be results focused (R), meaning that what is being measured is focused on the end product rather than the bare numbers. Finally, outcomes should be timely (T), meaning there is a specific timeline for the outcomes (Association of College & Research Libraries, n.d.).

A tool specifically suited to technology outcomes is the Impact Survey, which is funded by the Bill and Melinda Gates Foundation and exists to help measure how library patrons use public computers and the Internet in libraries. The tool is free, so any library can conduct its own survey to help advocate for more tech-focused funding or to help decide where to use limited resources. The Impact Survey can help your library find some indicators with which to measure. In the "Setting Targets" section you found benchmarks, and indicators help you decide if you have reached these benchmarks. Perhaps your desired outcome is increasing the digital literacy of 10 percent of your yearly library visitors. Some of the indicators might be the number of tech training opportunities, the percentage of students who feel more confident in their skills after attending a training session, and average attendance at tech training programs. Utilize these tools and measures at your disposal to ensure that your library is providing the best possible service to your community (Impact Survey, n.d.).

AFFORDABLE ALTERNATIVES

Fortunately, measuring data can mostly involve your staff using free tools. If anything, being a little overzealous in evaluation and data collection at your library is likely to equate to ultimate cost savings. Finding efficiencies and discovering the successes and failures of the services your library provides make your library a great steward of public funding. In terms of getting started, using the EDGE Assessment to find benchmarks and the Impact Survey to determine whether you have reached those benchmarks is fantastic (and free!). From there, you are simply interpreting data and deciding whether you've reached your goals.

7

The Future of Technology Services in Libraries

- Bookless Libraries
- Is Retail Really Our Enemy?
- What Is the Boundary for Technology Help?
- How Far Should We Travel for Tech Help?
- Future Staffing Thoughts
- Bluetooth Beacon Technology
- Coding
- Computer Classes and Job Skills
- Open Source
- Teaching and Learning
- Tor Nodes
- Beta Technology and Circulating Devices
- Library as Internet Service Provider
- One Last Word

Predicting the future is difficult. It is one of the reasons you wouldn't want to be a meteorologist, especially in the case of the famously unpredictable weather in the author's home state of Colorado. When it comes to predicting technology trends, that is even more difficult. Before the ubiquity of the iPhone, who would have predicted that the majority of the population would be walking around with tiny Wi-Fi enabled computers in our pockets? Pictures of people in wearable technology or virtual reality headsets may look silly or even dystopian to us now, but who is to say that these things will not become the norm down the line? Keeping this in mind, let's spend this chapter bouncing ideas off the wall that people have suggested that might be applicable to libraries of the future, or even today's libraries. Just promise not to make fun of yours truly five years from now for the prediction that everyone will be walking around with personal selfie drones by then.

BOOKLESS LIBRARIES

When e-books and e-reader sales were rising, some in the media predicted the death of the paper book and, by extension, the death of libraries. In reality, this has not been the case. Paper book sales are healthy, and libraries remain essential centers of many communities. However, there is something to be said about a bookless library. BiblioTech in San Antonio, Texas, is just that. The library is outfitted with computers, a café, and devices and laptops for checkout. Those who are looking for a good read can borrow a digital title and check out an e-reader for home use (Nawotka, 2014). As mentioned in chapter 4, the Denver Public Library system has come to the conclusion that it needs to change to a similar model as a result of a dilemma. DPL is a network of a few dozen libraries throughout the metro area, many of which are small neighborhood branches. These branches have lost some of their usefulness to their community because they tend to have very small collections to browse, and much of their circulation comes from holds couriered from larger branches. In light of this, a tech center outfitted with computers, devices, and meeting space is likely to better fit the community's needs. (Although those with transportation limitations may still use the branches to pick up books reserved online.)

An interesting benefit of the bookless library is that it provides a better environment for Wi-Fi. Frustratingly, environmental features found in most libraries make them less conducive to the ideal spread of a Wi-Fi signal. Wi-Fi is spread throughout a space using radio waves, and materials like metal can block and even reflect signals (Rothman, n.d.). What are most libraries chock full of? Metal stacks full of books, making it difficult to provide maximal Wi-Fi coverage. A bookless tech center would obviously be free of this issue!

IS RETAIL REALLY OUR ENEMY?

One of Arapahoe Libraries' goals has been to provide tech services that are comparable to if not better than the help one can get at retail spaces like Best Buy or the Apple Store. When a patron comes in and says, "I was about to take this to the Apple Store, but can you take a look first?," the goal has been reached! Retail tech help certainly has a place for consumers, but why not run your problem by your local library tech specialist first for free? The assistance in a retail store can be biased—for example, a simple question or assistance on your device may lead to an unnecessary purchase; many of these folks are salespeople, after all. Also, the skill level and quality of service from staff are often inconsistent. Technology help at your library is guaranteed to be unbiased, as libraries by nature cannot endorse one product over another.

About two years into the technology specialist service at Arapahoe Libraries, the library started hearing that the local Sprint phone store and a few local Best Buy stores were referring customers to the library for technology help. Although at both stores employees have a limited capacity for walk-in technology help, their bottom line is ultimately sales. Therefore, they saw fit to send customers to the library to receive more in-depth, one-on-one help. Perhaps libraries and retail stores do not necessarily have to be rivals. There is room for a potential partnership or at least a discussion with local electronics store managers about ways that both places might be able to help each other.

WHAT IS THE BOUNDARY FOR TECHNOLOGY HELP?

This brings up the dilemma of just how far libraries are willing to go for tech help. Many libraries have waivers for helping with any sort of personal device to avoid liability should something go wrong. One way to anticipate this issue is to have a standing agenda item at every meeting called "boundaries." This is a chance for staff to discuss specific situations that have arisen that struck them as perhaps bending too far to help someone or a request from a patron that was perhaps unreasonable. Examples are library patrons expecting a technology specialist to sit down with them to write a résumé from start to finish or who simply demand too much time and cause issues when other patrons walk in needing help. The boundary does not have to be a hard and fast line; these discussions help it retain fluidity.

As library tech help becomes more well known and popular and requests become more complex, people may start bringing in their PC towers and laptops for in-depth troubleshooting. While this may strike some as far beyond what libraries can and should offer, so long as the library has the resources to help, to the extent that we can without damaging the device and as long as liability has been accounted for either with a verbal agreement or a signed form, it's at least worth trying.

Keep in mind that library policy should always be about teaching people with or about technology. Do not allow people to simply drop off their laptops at your desks and say "please upgrade this to Windows 10" and walk away. If this is the direction the service is moving in your library, you can hire technology specialists with computer certifications to troubleshoot computers while educating the user on what she or he is doing. Or explore the possibility of a library-funded community PC repair service. New York Public Library offers Wi-Fi hot spots for in-home use to those in need, so it is not outside the realm of possibility to think of a public library offering a similar service but with PC repair (New York Public Library, 2015).

HOW FAR SHOULD WE TRAVEL FOR TECH HELP?

If providing technology help is a convenience to library patrons, why not find ways to help remotely for even more convenience? It can be difficult to reach patrons with Internet issues at home or homebound patrons with an in-library walk-up tech service. Some libraries, like the Putnam County Public Library in Indiana, do in fact provide in-home technology help for homebound or disabled patrons (Carson & Asbock, 2015). Bookmobiles also help widen the field of technology help libraries can provide by heading to retirement homes and community centers far from library branches. What about taking these steps a little further, what about a tech specialist who could remotely access a home computer to see exactly what the patron sees? Remote access is convenient and could reach many more patrons even more efficiently than in-home visits and bookmobiles do. There are certainly some challenges involved, like trusting the library to "see" your home computer and the basic technology competence the home user would need to be able to start a remote session with a library technology specialist. If considering actual in-home visits, you also want to first take into account the liability issues regarding both protecting staff and protecting the devices they are working on. Microsoft offers a service called remote assistance support and tackles some of these concerns via a liability agreement and a user-friendly interface that walks the user through the entire process (Microsoft, 2016). Modifying this agreement and taking some cues from Microsoft could help you reach an entirely new patron base and offer a level of customer service yet to be seen in library technology help.

FUTURE STAFFING THOUGHTS

As libraries begin offering STEM programming like coding to their patrons, they need to find ways to either hire or find people with the tech know-how to deliver this knowledge. A common concern heard in presentations or conversations about STEM programming is staff training and knowledge. It is unrealistic to expect library staff to completely master a coding language like Ruby in order to be able to teach a class. It is unrealistic to ask a library employee to become conversant enough in music recording to produce professional-sounding, full band recordings. However, it is not unrealistic to ask staff to be okay with learning alongside patrons or to ask staff to gain a basic understanding of makerspace and STEM tools. More often than not, it is more of a confidence issue with technology. Program hosts have to be comfortable with not being the experts, and as long as they are up front about this fact with program attendees, there is no problem. On the flip side, libraries can seek out tech-savvy paid staff or volunteers. If you do not have the skills in-house to teach the content you want to, find them! You would be surprised at how many tech-savvy individuals both inside and outside the library field want to work as technology specialists.

A study of the future of the master's in library science (MLS) degree, which the majority of professional library jobs require, identified problems in the current market and skills new MLS graduates need to have (Bertot & Sarin, 2015). These qualities should sound very familiar, as they are a few of the qualities listed for ideal tech specialist candidates in chapter 3. These qualities include adaptability, creativity, and tech savvy. The constantly changing nature of technology, and by proxy of their jobs, requires tech specialist staff to be incredibly adaptable. It is not uncommon to encounter a tech problem never before seen in an average tech specialist's shift. Creativity comes with STEM activities and makerspaces, where technology specialists are tasked with creating an environment of informal learning through teaching and creating themselves. It takes a creative mind to think of various workarounds and solutions to a tech problem. Finally, the term "tech savvy" may be self-explanatory, but consider it more as a state of mind. With some confidence and experience, you can embrace the idea of "tech savviness" without really feeling that you have learned everything. Based on studies like these and with new graduates entering the workforce, libraries will naturally move toward being staffed by individuals with the new standard of skills. Arapahoe Libraries have already seen the benefit of hiring for these qualities. A telltale sign is that technology specialists tend to be popular candidates for internal job promotions. Their combination of passion for public library service and built-in comfort and skill with technology makes them ideal for many internal positions.

BLUETOOTH BEACON TECHNOLOGY

Some libraries are using Bluetooth beacon technology for in-house marketing and promotion. The technology allows a smartphone with an accompanying app to receive a location-specific message. For example, the Orange County Library System tried it near the front door, where patrons would line up before the library opened on Tuesdays. Tuesday was the day new DVDs were released and always resulted in a line of early bird patrons outside the front door, so OCLS put in a beacon that sends out a message to each smartphone user in line about what is newly in stock that day. The Mount Pleasant Public Library integrated this technology with its ILS so users can receive messages specific to them about their items being ready when they're near the checkout desk. Yet another library in Europe uses beacons for a self-guided tour of the library for new users.

This technology has many exciting applications in libraries. Chapter 4 noted the usefulness of communicating which services happen where and guiding the user's eye to the tech bar or different service point. One of the best parts of this technology is personalizing promotional messages for the user. It is unrealistic to promote everything to everyone, so this allows a location-specific promotional message for, say, a library user who spends a lot of her time in the graphic novel section. Ideally, this service would have an opt-in and opt-out feature for users concerned about their privacy or who are simply uninterested. Regardless, in an increasingly smartphone-heavy world, this technology could be a boon to libraries, a subtle nudge to passersby to try a new service without plastering your library with excessive signage (Dempsey, 2016).

CODING

Coding is becoming an increasingly important life skill. Initiatives like Code Louisville and Denver Public Library's DevCamp have shown that libraries can lead the change by providing free coding education. Some predict that much like the gap in basic computer skills between baby boomers and younger generations, a similar gap will exist between the current generation and future generations who learn coding in school. There seems to be quite a bit of support for coding initiatives as well. A 2016 Pew study found that "80% of those ages 16 and older say libraries should 'definitely' offer programs to teach people, including kids and senior citizens, how to use digital tools like computers and smartphones" (Horrigan, 2016). There are few digital tools that are more valuable to teach children than coding; it may become a skill just as necessary to understand our world as basic reading literacy. Much as libraries have fulfilled the need for greater computer skills among baby boomers via computer classes and technology help, libraries can pitch in to help raise coding literacy for this potential future.

COMPUTER CLASSES AND JOB SKILLS

Today, adults tend to come to computer classes at the library seeking relevant job skills to bolster their résumés. In light of this, many libraries teach Microsoft Office products so that attendees can list Excel or Word proficiency among their skills. However, in today's workplace, basic computing skills with spreadsheets and text documents are a general expectation rather than a specific skills. Jada Graves (2012) of *US News* recommends leaving them off a résumé altogether for this very reason. Libraries need to change their computer class curriculum to meet the needs of their patrons who may not know what the most desirable computer skills are in the current job market. Teaching computer literacy, including the Office suite, still has a place for those in need of basic computer help, but libraries can do much more to educate their patrons and teach them desirable and relevant job skills like cloud storage, coding, and image manipulation to gain an edge in the working world.

OPEN SOURCE

Along with improving computer class curriculum, libraries can do more to support and promote open source software. Teaching computing skills on a free software suite like LibreOffice or the suite of Google products could be more helpful to library patrons than teaching the standard Microsoft Office suite. Many library patrons seeking basic computer help are likely among those in the digital divide and lack the finances to own a personal computer or software. Many smaller rural libraries in Colorado had patrons fitting this description, so the Colorado State Library teamed up with the CTC at the Denver Public Library to give these smaller libraries open source tools. The CTC loaded Linux, a free open source operating system, on donated laptops and installed a number of maker-friendly open source software, like the image manipulation program GIMP and audiorecording software Audacity (Library Learning & Creation Center, n.d.).

An advantage of teaching open source software to library patrons is that it equips them to use free tools accessible from anywhere. When someone of lower socioeconomic status purchases a personal computer, already having a knowledge base of free and open source software gives that person immense cost savings on software and a great starting knowledge of these tools for her or his professional and personal lives. Photoshop is prohibitively expensive, but teaching library patrons GIMP and its Photoshop-esque capabilities could show them the power of open source. Admittedly, teaching open source software can be more difficult, as it tends to have less user-friendly interfaces than paid software, but giving patrons the ability to practice on their own for free on either a personal device or a library computer is more than worth the trouble.

TEACHING AND LEARNING

Libraries have long been educational institutions, whether through formal classes or simply via access to information. With the increasingly changing landscape of libraries, those focused more on digital content and in-library activities and less on physical material circulation are seeing trends in varieties of learning in this environment. STEM and the maker movement lend themselves especially well to informal learning, the act of tinkering and exploring exactly what interests the user. The Institute of Museum and Library Services (IMLS) reports that informal learning is important in early childhood. A simple craft table or blocks in a museum or library can encourage tinkering and help make connections in young minds. The IMLS (2013) proposes a concerted effort in standardizing learning initiatives in these institutions to offer a more formalized approach. Since this format works well for youth and the maker movement, perhaps it is worth reevaluating our traditional teaching methods for other instruction that goes on in the library. Making the importance of informal learning for children known to parents and the rest of the community is a necessary push for library communities as a whole so that they will be recognized as centers for this type of educational activity.

A massive open online course (MOOC) is free, open access education on the Web. As a learning format, MOOCs are rising in popularity as alternatives to classrooms or lectures for education in libraries. They are most often self-led, though they are occasionally accompanied by a monthly or weekly in-person class to check for understanding. *Library Journal* reported in 2013 that public libraries could benefit in a number of ways from MOOCs, from simply providing the requisite Internet access to hosting one and encouraging participation (Schwartz, 2013). MOOCs in libraries are ideal for any skill that builds upon itself or cannot be covered in a single class. Most often, coding and Web design are subjects that have met these criteria. In any case, MOOCs are a fantastic way to encourage both digital and physical library use, especially when paired with an educational library resource like Treehouse or Lynda.

While we are on the subject of self-led education in public libraries, why not consider community-led meet-ups? In many cities, Meetup.com is a fantastic resource to bring together people with similar interests. Often, hosts just need a venue to make their meet-up happen. Public libraries should encourage these gatherings and proactively find ways to help support them. For example, the content management system WordPress hosts happy hours that gather together developers who stand to benefit from trading ideas and discussing common issues. The library could use this as a resource to promote tech education through Lynda or simply to promote meeting space and Wi-Fi use. As mentioned in the coding section, it's unreasonable to expect library employees to learn to code, but hosting and encouraging coding meet-ups is a great way to make those connections to perhaps lessen the impact on your library staff.

TOR NODES

In the age of the National Security Agency (NSA) and with the Patriot Act (2001) still fresh in the minds of Americans, the issue of privacy in libraries is as relevant as ever. Libraries have long been harbingers of intellectual freedom and supporters of access to any and all information. However, as the Internet becomes dominated by private companies like Google and Amazon, which regularly gather user data without our having any say in the matter, questions arise about just how private our Internet browsing is. Why does that matter to the average user? An example of one of the most immediate concerns is that e-commerce sites like Office Depot have admitted to changing prices offered online based on an individual user's browsing history and location (Valentino-Devries, Singer-Vine, & Soltani, 2012). This practice may appear as "just doing business," but it sets a precedent that can feel invasive and unfair. Many people simply do not want their information to be so readily available to the interests of corporations.

The Library Freedom Project (libraryfreedomproject.org) has taken steps toward a potential future for private Internet access. It maintains that the best way to uphold the public library's philosophy of privacy is to use a Tor network for Internet access. A Tor network is made up of a number of privately owned servers and nodes that improve one's privacy and security while using the Internet. The servers are volunteer run, and a secure virtual connection is used, making Internet browsing and information sharing on public networks safer and more private (Tor, n.d.). A number of institutions and individuals use the technology and have joined with the Library Freedom Project. This extra layer of protection is used by crime victims who need to keep a low profile, branches of the military, and journalists gathering information from sensitive sources. Libraries need to consider this possibility as they become more and more popular places for Internet access and as a result places where sensitive information might be shared over the network.

BETA TECHNOLOGY AND CIRCULATING DEVICES

You may have seen news stories and press releases about libraries circulating unusual items or devices. Some mention tool libraries, which allow library card holders to take a shovel home to use for a single-use project. Other libraries circulate museum or zoo passes that serve for free or discounted trips to these locations. On the technology side of things, a number of tech devices have started circulating. In 2015 the New York Public Library began circulating Wi-Fi hot spots specifically for those without in-home wireless Internet. Other libraries have followed suit by circulating hot spots themselves, but without any restrictions. Another tech lending innovation was started by Kansas City Public Library, which launched a Software Lending Library in 2014, utilizing the city's speedy gigabit Internet connection to allow home users to remotely access software like Adobe Photoshop free of charge (Enis, 2013). Some people may see the lending of these nontraditional items as a breach of library protocol, but in reality, these items are as in line with library philosophies about access and information as anything else a library circulates.

Arapahoe Libraries circulate nontraditional devices but have also expanded that service into a beta technology program. Beta technology can be defined as not quite "market ready" technology. Companies occasionally release beta technology versions to test in a small market. Arapahoe Libraries have acquired Google Glass, the Oculus Rift Development Kits, and the Microsoft HoloLens for this initiative. The idea is to expose the public to what tends to be expensive, hard-to-find technology and educate them on the future possibilities available. Similar to the thinking behind makerspaces and tool lending, the idea is to provide access to tools and technology that the average library patron may not otherwise be able to afford or access. Live demonstrations, outreach events, and one-on-one appointments allow the public to have supervised access to these items. Although investment in beta technology can be risky and expensive, Arapahoe Libraries have found it to be fantastic for marketing and technology education in general. This model has the potential to establish libraries as the technology showrooms of the future, conducting live demonstrations of technology on the floor.

LIBRARY AS INTERNET SERVICE PROVIDER

Wireless Internet access is essentially non-negotiable for the modern public library. System administrators and other library information technology workers around the country are experiencing an arms race in increasing Internet speeds and improving hardware like access points and routers to keep up with demand. They increase the Internet speeds when they become available, and the public uses more data and puts more strain on the network. Some of the most popular Web sites among the public by far are YouTube and Netflix. Playing or streaming video from sites like these is a huge burden on Internet speed and bandwidth. Now imagine an entire library of users playing videos or streaming simultaneously. It results in a slow, overburdened Internet connection. Therefore, libraries are always working with their ISPs to maintain the best speeds possible in their area for whatever fits their budget. However, these ISPs are third-party corporations that do not have an inherent interest in helping libraries; after all, they need to make a profit. Adding to the problem is that there are usually only one or two ISPs to choose from in any given area, negating the need for these companies to have particularly competitive pricing, good customer service, or timely maintenance. It's frustrating for libraries to have to be beholden to external companies to provide something so integral to their existence.

In this light, if the author of this book were a wealthy philanthropist (or much more likely, if he had the ear of a wealthy philanthropist), he would position the public library as the community's ISP. Of course this would take an incredible amount of labor, making an entire city's or community's network from scratch, but the library could provide in-home wireless Internet service free of charge. It makes sense with the library's philosophy of free and open access to information. Net neutrality would be of no concern, as the ALA (n.d.) adamantly opposes any sort of "fast lane" for specific Web sites. It would help break the monopoly that ISPs have in many areas of the United States and bring the public library into the 21st century as not a community resource, but a community utility. And this may not be as far-fetched as it sounds. Many European countries and some U.S. cities have provided free wireless Internet to residents, a municipal wireless network. These networks are often composed of a number of wireless hot spots all stitched together under one service set identifier (SSID), and many pilot projects have started with already established free wireless areas in municipal buildings and public libraries, so it is a logical extension from what libraries already offer.

ONE LAST WORD

In short, the future of technology in libraries is bright. Common post-interview questions from potential technology specialist applicants are: How new is this service, and how secure will I be in my job? The answer to both is easy: there are few libraries out there that are not growing or at least maintaining their technology offerings, whether offering more complex digital tools along with education, changing their spaces to reflect the technology needs of their populations, or starting technology specialist teams of their own. In the nascent years of technology specialist service at Arapahoe Libraries, the team grew from about 6 FTE to about 8 FTE, with ever-increasing demand for more. The CTC at the Denver Public Library started out with 3.5 FTE in 2011 and is up to 13.5 FTE in 2017. Public schools are starting to offer STEM tracks, and STEM-specific schools are popping up across the country. Technology education is as important as ever in society, and it is heartening to see public libraries leading the charge. The next innovations and forward-thinking initiatives are in your hands!

Appendix A: Putnam County Public Library Technology Plan

TECHNOLOGY MISSION STATEMENT

The Putnam County Public Library endeavors to be a community leader in helping to close the digital divide by being a central place for patrons to access tools and information while developing essential digital literacy skills. The Library will provide knowledgeable and trained staff who curate electronic resources, train and guide patrons in their use, educate and stimulate the public as to the role of technology in their lives, and use technology to do their own jobs more effectively.

PLAN OBJECTIVE

The library remains committed to building and maintaining a robust technology program that includes equitable access to myriad forms of information and content creation tools as well as providing an engaging and supportive environment in which to explore and experiment with new technologies. This technology plan will serve as a guide in the library's continual efforts to further integrate current and future consumer technologies into the daily library experience of its patrons and staff.

PART 1:

Environment and Background

Infrastructure

The Putnam County Public Library has made significant improvements in its technology infrastructure over the past 2 years. At the start of 2014, the library maintained a fiber optic line offering 10mbps download speeds and 2 dedicated wireless access points. In June of 2014, the library's 10mbps fiber optic line was increased to 70mbps (ENA). Management of the wireless network was subsequently outsourced to ENA Air, including the installation/upgrade and maintenance of 4 new wireless access points. A network assessment report was then commissioned and executed in November of 2014 (Telemagen) and has since served to guide much of the improvement and expansion of the library's internal network.

Automation: Polaris Integrated Library System (Innovative Interfaces Incorporated)

PCPL is entering its 10th year with the Polaris integrated library system (a product of Innovative Interfaces Incorporated since its acquisition in 2014). Regular upgrades to Polaris have been maintained since its adoption in 2006. All circulating collections, including e-content accessed through Overdrive .com, are cataloged and searchable via the library's instance of Polaris.

Website

In September of 2014, the library launched a new and vastly-improved website. PCPL commissioned WynWay Technologies to design and maintain the new website, which focuses heavily on ease of use (for both patrons and staff) as well as aesthetic appeal. Built using the WordPress platform, the site allows for easy uploading of library content including programing events and other calendar updates, featured collections and services, engaging multimedia files representing library activities and plans, staff and library board information and meetings minutes, and much more. The website is hosted remotely and is serviced by WynWay Technologies and 25/7 Consulting. The library purchased a customized and simplified domain name for the new website.

The following is an outline of the library's current local and remote services including network hardware/software paradigms and outsourced network services:

- **Network environment including local network hardware and software paradigm(s)**

- **Putnam County Public Library maintains a Microsoft Windows Server Network Domain.**
  1. Network Infrastructure Hardware
     1. WatchGuard Firebox Firewall Appliance
     2. Dell 48 Port Gigabit Network Core Switch
     3. Microsoft Windows Domain
        1. Microsoft Windows Domain Controller
        2. Microsoft Windows Backup Domain Controller
        3. Polaris Production Server
     4. Expandable 4 terabyte network attached storage
  2. Server Software
     1. Polaris Library Systems Automated Library Software
     2. Cassie (virtualized)
     3. Public computer patron authentication, print management, statistics collection, automatic reservations and waiting lists.
     4. Deep Freeze (virtualized)
     5. Protects all public access computers preventing permanent configuration changes.
     6. Teamviewer
     7. Teamviewer provides remote access to computers and servers to IT management staff.
  3. Specialized Client/Cloud Software
     1. Windows 10 Pro
     2. Microsoft Office
     3. Google Apps for Work
     4. Adobe Creative Suite 6
     5. Polaris Client
     6. ESET & Malwarebytes Antivirus
     7. WordPress
- **Current outsourced network services (who and what) and how they fit into the picture.**
  1. Network Infrastructure (Telemagen)
  2. Telemagen is a local Network Engineering firm that supplements the expertise of library Information Technology Manager and lends support during special projects or rollouts that require greater staffing than the library can supply.
  3. Website Design and Website Hosting (25/7 Consulting)
  4. Regular website and database updates are maintained by library staff with some of the more complicated or time intensive web site duties outsourced to a local student run web design company called 25/7 Consulting.

5. Wireless Access is managed by Education Networks of America
6. Network and Telephone Wiring is currently outsourced to local wiring company 12 Point Telecom

Staff Workflow and Communication

In conjunction with the website upgrade in September of 2014, the library migrated from a locally-hosted email solution to Gmail. This move included the adoption of Google Drive as the primary means for internal collaboration and communication. Weekly website updates and staff/department content uploads are also managed through the library's Google account.

2 Scanning, Copying, and Printing

All networked printers are leased and serviced through Ricoh. Additionally, each department maintains its own dedicated local printer for staff use. The library maintains 3 copier/scanner/printer machines for public use.

Telephone Services

The library contracts with MetroNet for its telephone services. 17 office phones (including 1 cordless phone) are used by library staff on a daily basis. 3 long distance business lines, 1 alarm line, and 1 elevator emergency call line are maintained through a monthly service contract with the carrier. The overall telephone system and contract are reviewed annually.

The Imagination Portal and Integrated Technology

In October of 2014, renovation of PCPL's Children's Department was completed and the doors to the newly-christened *Imagination Portal* were opened to the public. The central idea behind the new space was to provide a rich technological physical environment that engaged young patrons in the world of media and content around them while encouraging a sense of play and experimentation with technology not traditionally found in public libraries. The introduction of a variety of new computers (including Apple iMacs and HP touch screen all-in-one desktops), large screen television monitors, wireless projection tools, game consoles, and a MIDI-capable digital piano has since contributed to a sense of "digital playground" in the department. The hope was to provide open access to these tools while simultaneously demystifying much of the technology for parents and other patrons.

For many patrons, the daily library experience has significantly changed as a result of the integrated technology introduced in the Imagination Portal. The mere act of adding new computers has attracted large numbers of patrons to the space. More significantly, an open-access policy regarding installation of software has facilitated a tremendous increase in creative game-playing within the library. As a result, young patrons frequently come into the Imagination Portal for the express purpose of playing Minecraft and other online games/environments. Large touch-screen desktop computers now serve as PAC machines and allow for easier access to the library's online catalog.

Library programming has also expanded and diversified as a result of the new space and the technology therein. Video game nights have been very successful not only in helping to legitimize video games as a literary and artistic medium but also in bringing strong numbers of teens and "tweens" into the library, many of whom had never come to the library before. Basic coding and computer programming workshops have also been introduced, while digital creativity programs involving timeline editing skills and multimedia project management have been planned for later this year.

Technology Support and Instruction

In July 2014, the library began planning for a series of free and open technology classes for the public. The goal was to address aspects of the digital divide within Putnam County as it pertains to basic computing skills.

At the same time, the library introduced a new patron support service in the form of a technology help desk. Members of the Technology Department routinely staff the help desk (currently accessed through the Reference Desk and/or via email/phone) and post scheduled help desk hours on the library's website. Help desk support is provided both onsite (in the form of private consultations) and online/phone depending on circumstances. Patrons are encouraged to bring any computer or general technology questions or problems to the Help Desk and often bring malfunctioning hardware in for troubleshooting assistance.

Plans are currently in place to schedule remote help desk hours through the Outreach Department. The tech help desk has met with tremendous success. There is also a noted correlation between tech help desk interviews and attendance at library technology classes. The following is an outline of the staff and patron computing environment with regard to library-wide platforms, access paradigms, hardware peripherals, and user support/instruction:

- **Current staff and patron technology environment**
  1. Staff
     1. All library staff members have access to a Windows 10 workstation with Internet access and various local and cloud based productivity software.
     2. Select employees have access to laptops and/or tablet computers on an as needed basis.

      3. High Speed Wireless Internet Access

      4. Access to a mobile technology classroom consisting of 11 touch screen laptops, high definition short-throw digital projector, and mobile screen for library programming purposes.

      5. Access to high capacity color laser printing

  2. Patrons

      1. 24 public workstations with filtered internet access

      2. 6 touch screen all-in-one public access catalog workstations

      3. Access to high capacity color laser printing

      4. Community Help Desk

      5. Patrons have access to a computer technician to help diagnose and repair patron computer and electronics. Currently our Community Help Desk is only during specific hours, four days a week with a goal of expanding to all of the hours the library is open.

      6. Wireless Internet

      7. Our managed wifi service is a 70 gigabit per second 802.11 a/b/g/n and 802.11ac wireless service with seamless roaming between four different library access points.

- **Current/future technology training (staff) and education (public) program**

  1. Public Technology Education

  2. The library currently offers 14 public technology classes, in three class tracks, that are 2 hours long with a 10 minute break. For hands-on classes, registration is required to guarantee a workstation and limited to 10 students. Students will not be allowed to bring their own computers. All classes will be available to staff members either at the scheduled public time or one-on-one by appointment. Class Track 1: Computer Basics

      1. Introduction to Computers Part 1 (Hands-On)

      2. Introduction to Computers Part 2 (Hands-On)

      3. Introduction to Computers Part 3 (Hands-On)

      4. Introduction to Modern Operating Systems (Currently Windows 10) (Lecture Only)

  2. Class Track 2: Internet Basics

      1. Introduction to the Internet (Lecture Only)

      2. Safety and Security on the Internet (Lecture Only)

      3. Introduction to Social Networking (Lecture Only)

      4. Introduction to Cloud Computing (Lecture Only)

  3. Class Track 3: Productivity Tools

      1. Introduction to Word Processing (Hands-On)

      2. Advanced Word Processing (Hands-On)

      3. Introduction to Spreadsheets (Hands-On)

      4. Advanced Spreadsheets (Hands-On)

     5. Tablets and Smartphones (Lecture Only)

     6. Managing Your Digital Photos (Hands-On)

3. Employee Technology Professional Development

4. Employees are encouraged to attend the public technology classes to fill in gaps in their technology education. If an employee cannot, or prefers not to attend public classes, one-on-one training on any topic may be scheduled with the Information Technology staff. The following are regularly scheduled technology classes for staff members only.

     1. Annual Google Apps for Work class (Hands-On)

     2. Polaris ILS Training after every Polaris upgrade (approx. every 18 months) utilizing Polaris online training offerings and department heads.

Appendix B: Arapahoe Libraries Question Complexity Over Time Data

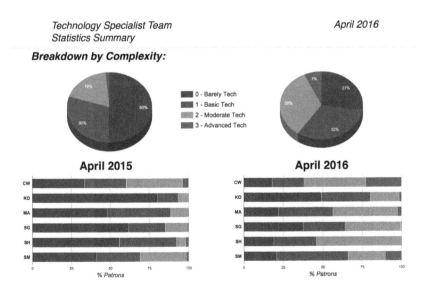

Technology Specialist Team
Statistics Summary

April 2016

Breakdown by Complexity:

0 - Barely Tech
1 - Basic Tech
2 - Moderate Tech
3 - Advanced Tech

April 2015

April 2016

Appendix C: Denver Public Library Project Card

Source: 3D printing and modeling basics. (2015, February 21). Retrieved December 9, 2016, from https://www.denverlibrary.org/ctc/3d-modeling-printing-and-basics

What is Tinkercad?

Tinkercad is an easy browser-based 3D design tool. You can pretty much design whatever you can imagine.

Getting Started in Tinkercad

1. navigate to **tinkercad.com**
2. Select the **Start Tinkering** button.
3. Create an account or sign in using **Google** or **Facebook.**
4. Start Making stuff!

The Tinkercad interface

This is your main design space. Here is where you will be creating the majority of your work on Tinkercad. The blue gridded area represents the build plate that is used by 3D printers. You will want to create your work on this plate.

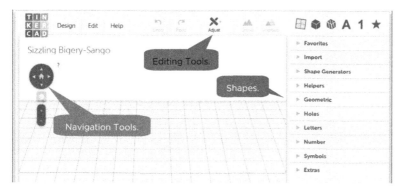

SHAPES You will primarily use Shapes to design your 3D object. Geometric includes most of the commonly used shapes.

NAVIGATION TOOLS These allow you to zoom in and out, rotate the screen, and shift your perspective around an object.

EDITING TOOLS This houses your **undo/redo** options, as well as **Adjust**, which lets you align objects to one another and mirror them. And don't forget about **Group** which lets you join multiple objects together so you can move them at the same time.

Manipulating Shapes

You can add a shape to the grid by clicking and dragging it, but then what can you do with it? You may have noticed all the funny little arrows and boxes around the shape? They do all kinds of stuff, like:

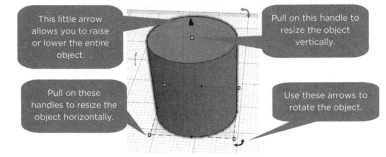

Grouping Shapes

You can group 2 or more shapes together with the Group button. Grouping means that what you do to one shape will also happen to the other (this includes resizing, moving, and rotating).

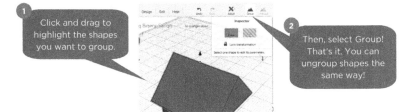

Saving/Downloading your Project

Your project will automatically save, but you may want to download it so it can be 3D printed!

Step 1: Select **Design**.

Step 2: Select **Download for 3D Printing.**

Step 3: Select **STL** as the file type.

Tinkercad keyboard shortcuts

Moving object(s)

⬆ / ➡ / ⬅ / ⬇	**Move** object(s) along X/Y
ctrl + ⬆ / ⬇	**Move** object(s) along Z
Shift + ⬆ / ➡ / ⬅ / ⬇	**×10 Nudge** along X/Y
ctrl + **Shift** + ⬆ / ⬇	**×10 Nudge** along Z

Keyboard + mouse shortcuts (press and hold kbd btn, then move mouse)

Alt + left mouse button	**Duplicate** object(s)
Shift + left mouse button	**Select** multiple object(s)
Shift + hold while roating	**45° roation**
Alt + hold *side handle*	**Scale (1D)**
Alt + hold *corner handle*	**Scale (2D)**
Shift + hold *corner handle*	**Scale (3D)**
Shift + **Alt** + hold *corner handle*	**Scale (3D)**
Shift + **Alt** + hold *top handle*	**Scale (3D)**
Shift + right mouse button	**Pan view**

Tinkercad mouse controls

Right Click: rotate the camera.

Shift + Right Click: pan the camera.

Left Click: move, size and select objects.

Mouse Wheel (roll): zoom in and out

Mouse Wheel (click): pan the camera.

idea**LAB** COMMUNITY **TECHNOLOGY** CENTER | 10 W 14ᵗʰ Ave Parkway
Denver, CO 80204 | 720.865.1706 | http://teens.denverlibrary.org/idealab

🔥 DENVER PUBLIC LIBRARY

More Tinkercad keyboard shortcuts!

General shortcuts

`ctrl` + `C`	**Copy** object(s)
`ctrl` + `V`	**Paste** object(s)
`ctrl` + `Z`	**Undo** action(s)
`ctrl` + `Shift` + `Z`	**Re-do** action(s)
`ctrl` + `G`	**Group** object(s)
`ctrl` + `shift` + `G`	**Un-group** object(s)
`ctrl` + `D`	**Duplicate** in-place
`ctrl` + `L`	**Lock** object(s)
`ctrl` + `A`	**Select** all object(s)
`Del`	**Delete** object(s)
`W`	**Workplane** toggle
`R`	**Ruler** toggle
`F`	**Fit view** to selected object(s)
`D`	**Drops** object(s) to work plane

WHERE TO GET MORE HELP:

Tinkercad Quest: Tinkercad.com is stuffed to the gills with lessons and 3D models to remix and use! Get learning!

Want Inspirations? Check out Thingiverse.com: Thingiverse is a thriving design community for discovering, making, and sharing 3D printable things . Most submissions are licensed under the Creative Commons so exploring, remixing and sharing are encouraged!

Print your masterpiece: Come to ideaLAB during lab hours to submit your print and see the 3D printers in action!

COMMUNITY **TECHNOLOGY** CENTER | 10 W 14ᵗʰ Ave Parkway
Denver, CO 80204 | 720.865.1706 | http://teens.denverlibrary.org/idealab

Appendix D: Arapahoe Libraries Tech Interaction Data Collection Form

Tech Specialist Patron Interactions

Duration

- < 5 minutes
- 5–10 minutes
- 10–30 minutes
- 30–60 minutes
- 60–90 minutes
- > 90 minutes

Time Began: _____
Optional—this will overwrite an inaccurate timestamp

 # Patrons _____

Referral

- Walk-up
- Staff handoff
- Appointment

- ○ Tech Program
- ○ Drop-in Demo
- ○ Other

Complexity

- ○ 0 - Barely Tech
- ○ 1 - Basic Tech
- ○ 2 - Moderate Tech
- ○ 3 - Advanced Tech

Category

- ○ General—"What's the tech bar?"
- ○ 3D Printer/Scanner/Design
- ○ Studio/Makerspace
- ○ Other Beta Tech (finch, drone, sphero . . .)
- ○ Library Digital Resources (e-books, databases, zinio, hoopla . . .)
- ○ Computer Help (word processing, Internet . . .)
- ○ Mobile Device Help (not related to library resources)
- ○ Other Library Tech (A/V, printer, fax, copier . . .)

More Information (if needed):

Appendix E: Arapahoe Libraries Tech Data Readout

Breakdown by Category:

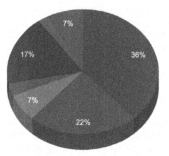 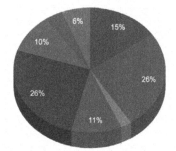

April 2015   **April 2016**

- 3D Printer/Scanner/Design
- Studio/Makerspace
- Other Beta Tech
- Library Digital Resources
- Computer Help
- Mobile Device Help
- Other Library Tech
- General - 'What's the tech bar?'

Breakdown by Complexity:

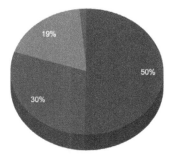 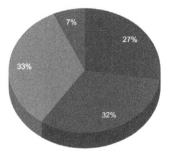

April 2015   April 2016

0 - Barely Tech

1 - Basic Tech

2 - Moderate Tech

3 - Advanced Tech

Breakdown by Referral Method:

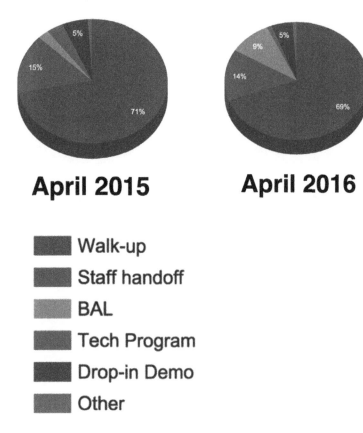

References

American Library Association (ALA). (n.d.). Network neutrality. Retrieved September 30, 2016, from http://www.ala.org/advocacy/telecom/netneutrality

American Library Association (ALA). (2014). Public library use: ALA library fact sheet 6. Retrieved September 2, 2016, from http://www.ala.org/tools/libfactsheets/alalibraryfactsheet06

Association of College & Research Libraries. (n.d.). What is a SMART objective? Retrieved September 30, 2016, from http://www.ala.org/acrl/aboutacrl/directoryofleadership/sections/is/iswebsite/projpubs/smartobjectives/whatisamartobjective

Bertot, J. C., Jaeger, P. T., & McClure, C. R. (2010). *Public libraries and the Internet.* Santa Barbara, CA: Libraries Unlimited.

Bertot, J. C., Jaeger, P. T., Wahl, E. E., & Sigler, K. I. (2011, August/September). Public libraries and the internet: An evolutionary perspective. *Library Technology Reports, 9.*

Bertot, J. C., & Sarin, L. (2015, February 26). The future of MLIS: Rethinking librarian education. *American Libraries.* Retrieved August 29, 2016, from https://americanlibrariesmagazine.org/2015/02/26/the-future-of-mls/

Bizzle, B., & Flora, M. (2015). *Start a revolution: Stop acting like a library.* Chicago: ALA Editions.

Bolt, N. (n.d.). Seven major trends facing public libraries. Retrieved September 2, 2016, from https://ilceig.files.wordpress.com/2013/08/trends-in-public-library-service.pdf

Britton, L. (2012, July/August). A fabulous labaratory [*sic*]: The makerspace at Fayetteville Free Library. *Public Libraries Online.* Retrieved August 29, 2016, from http://publiclibrariesonline.org/2012/10/a-fabulous-labaratory-the-makerspace-at-fayetteville-free-library/.

Brodkin, J. (2015, February 4). Open Internet, but a lack of competition among providers. *The New York Times.* Retrieved August 29, 2016, from http://www

.nytimes.com/roomfordebate/2015/02/04/regulate-internet-providers/open
-internet-but-a-lack-of-competition-among-providers

Carson, G., & Asbock, M. (2015). Putnam County Public Library technology plan. Retrieved September 3, 2016, from http://pcpl21.org/library/technology-plan/

Chant, I. (2015, May 15). LFPL trains tech talent: Library plays key role in Code Louisville. *Library Journal*, 17–18.

Chuang, T. (2015, July 10). Denver Library wins big award for teen tech-developer camps [blog]. Retrieved August 29, 2016, from http://blogs.denverpost.com/tech/2015/07/10/denver-library-wins-big-award-for-kids-tech-developer-camps/17822/

Clark, L., & Perry, K. A. (2015, December). After access: Libraries & digital empowerment. Retrieved July 7, 2015, from http://www.ala.org/advocacy/sites/ala.org.advocacy/files/content/ALA DI After Access_final_12 17 15.pdf

Columbus, L. (2014, September 15). Demand for 3D printing skills is accelerating globally. *Forbes*. Retrieved August 29, 2016, from http://www.forbes.com/sites/louiscolumbus/2014/09/15/demand-for-3d-printing-skills-is-accelerating-globally/#23f17a974cf7

Columbus Museum of Art. (2014, June 18). Homago, connected learning, and teen after school programming. Retrieved August 29, 2016, from https://www.columbusmuseum.org/homago-connected-learning-teen-school-programming/

Dempsey, K. (2016, May). Bluetooth beacons are starting to shine in libraries. *Info Today*, 29–31.

Department for Professional Workers, AFL-CIO. (2011). Library workers: Facts & figures. Fact sheet 2011. Retrieved September 2, 2016, from http://ala-apa.org/files/2012/03/Library-Workers-2011.pdf

Digital Inclusion Survey. (2015). Interactive map. Retrieved August 29, 2016, from http://digitalinclusion.umd.edu/content/interactive-map

Dowd, N. (2013, March 7). The LibraryAware Community Survey: Marketing our libraries. *Library Journal*. Retrieved September 3, 2016, from http://l.libraryjournal.com/2013/03/marketing/the-libraryaware-community-survey-marketing-our-libraries-library-marketing/#_

EDGE. (2015). Digital literacy. Retrieved September 30, 2016, from http://www.libraryedge.org/benchmarks/community-value/digital-literacy

Enis, M. (2013, September 13). Kansas City PL to launch software lending library pilot. *Library Journal*. Retrieved September 30, 2016, from http://lj.libraryjournal.com/2013/09/technology/kansas-city-pl-to-launch-software-lending-library-pilot/

Farmer, L. S. (2011). *Instructional design for librarians and information professionals*. New York: Neal-Schuman.

File, T., & Ryan, C. (2014, November). Computer and Internet use in the United States: 2013. Retrieved August 29, 2016, from https://www.census.gov/history/pdf/2013computeruse.pdf

Gerding, S. K. (2007). *The accidental technology trainer: A guide for libraries*. Medford, NJ: Information Today.

Goldin, R. (2015, August 19). Causation vs correlation. Retrieved August 29, 2016, from http://www.stats.org/causation-vs-correlation/

Graves, J. A. (2012, May 24). 4 job "skills" to leave off a resume. *U.S. News & World Report*. Retrieved September 3, 2016, from http://money.usnews.com/money/careers/articles/2012/05/24/4-job-skills-to-leave-off-a-resume

Hardy, L., & Griebel, R. (2014, December). Rethinking the present, designing the future: Calgary Public Library. *Felicitier, 60*(6), 29–31.

Herrera-Viedma, E., & Lopez-Gijon, J. (2013, March 22). Libraries' social role in the information age. SCIENCE, *339*, 1382.

Hopwood, J. (2012, August/September). Initiating STEM learning in libraries. *Children and Libraries, 53–55.*

Horrigan, J. B. (2016, September 9). Library usage and engagement. Retrieved September 24, 2016, from http://www.pewinternet.org/2016/09/09/library-usage -and-engagement/

Houghton-Jan, S. (2010). *Technology training in libraries.* New York: Neal-Schuman.

Impact survey. (n.d.). Retrieved September 30, 2016, from https://impactsurvey.org/

Information Policy and Access Center. (2012). Library e-government and employment services and challenges. Retrieved August 29, 2016, from http://www.ala .org/research/sites/ala.org.research/files/content/initiatives/plftas/2011_2012 /egovsvcs-ipac.pdf

Institute of Museum and Library Services (IMLS). (2002). Evaluation resources. Retrieved September 30, 2016, from https://www.imls.gov/research-evaluation /evaluation-resources

Institute of Museum and Library Services (IMLS). (2013, June). Growing young minds: How museums and libraries create lifelong learners. Retrieved September 3, 2016, from https://www.imls.gov/assets/1/AssetManager/GrowingYoung Minds.pdf

Institute of Museum and Library Services (IMLS). (2014, December). Public libraries in the United States survey. Retrieved September 2, 2016, from https://www .imls.gov/assets/1/AssetManager/PLS_FY2012.pdf

Is tech support professional work? (2009, November 11). *Library Journal.* Retrieved February 27, 2017, from http://lj.libraryjournal.com/blogs/annoyedlibrarian/2009/11/11/is-tech-support-professional-work/

Johnson, R. (2011, November 21). What I learned building the Apple Store. Retrieved September 3, 2016, from https://hbr.org/2011/11/what-i-learned -building-the-ap

Kastner, A. (2015, October 12). The personal touch. *Library Journal.* Retrieved September 3, 2016, from http://lj.libraryjournal.com/2015/10/public-services/the -personal-touch-readers-advisory/

Kravets, D. (2011, June 3). U.N. report declares Internet access a human right. Retrieved August 29, 2016, from https://www.wired.com/2011/06/internet-a -human-right

LaRue, J. (2016, May 16). Indyreads: Australia's new e-content platform. Retrieved February 24, 2017, from https://americanlibrariesmagazine.org/blogs/e-content /indyreads-australias-new-e-content-platform/

Library Learning & Creation Center. (n.d.). Digital creation software. Retrieved September 30, 2016, from http://create.coloradovirtuallibrary.org/digital-creation -software/

Lib2Gov. (n.d.). Community needs assessment. Retrieved August 29, 2016, from http://lib2gov.org/e-government-basics/community-needs-assessment

Lucas-Alfieri, D. (2015). *Marketing the 21st century library: The time is now* (1st ed.). Witney, Oxford: Chandos Publishing.

Mathews, B., & Soistmann, L. A. (2016). *Encoding space: Shaping learning environments that unlock human potential*. Chicago: Association of College and Research Libraries.

Matthews, J. R. (2004). *Measuring for results: The dimensions of public library effectiveness*. Westport, CT: Libraries Unlimited.

Meldrem, J. A., Mardis, L. A., & Johnson, C. (2005, April 7). Redesign your reference desk: Get rid of it! ACRL, 305–311.

Microsoft. (2016). Receive remote assistance support from Microsoft. Retrieved September 3, 2016, from https://support.microsoft.com/en-us/gp/eahelp

Minnesota Public Libraries' return on investment. (2011, December). Retrieved September 30, 2016, from http://melsa.org/melsa/assets/File/Library_final.pdf

Mobile technology fact sheet. (2013, December 27). Retrieved August 29, 2016, from http://www.pewinternet.org/fact-sheets/mobile-technology-fact-sheet/ [Page no longer accessible; most recent relevant study is found at http://www.pewinternet.org/fact-sheet/mobile/.]

Molaro, A., & White, L. L. (2015). *The library innovation toolkit: Ideas, strategies, and programs*. Chicago: ALA Editions.

Nawotka, E. (2014, January 18). It's here: A library with nary a book. *The New York Times*. Retrieved September 3, 2016, from http://www.nytimes.com/2014/01/19/us/its-here-a-library-with-nary-a-book.html?_r=1

New York Public Library. (2015). Library HotSpot. Retrieved September 3, 2016, from http://hotspot.nypl.org/

New York Public Library/NYPL TechConnecct. (2016). What's your tech profile? Retrieved September 10, 2016, from https://sites.google.com/a/nypl.org/techconnect-test-site/

Olanoff, D. (2015, July 15). President Obama: "The Internet is not a luxury, it is a necessity." Retrieved August 29, 2016, from https://techcrunch.com/2015/07/15/internet-for-everyone/#.tgyblg:yL0D

Public Libraries & the Internet. (n.d.). Digital literacy & public libraries. Retrieved August 29, 2016, from http://www.plinternetsurvey.org/analysis/public-libraries-and-digital-literacy

Public library funding & technology access study 2011–2012. (2012, June/July). Retrieved August 29, 2016, from http://www.ala.org/research/sites/ala.org.research/files/content/initiatives/plftas/2011_2012/plftas12_execsummary.pdf

Rainie, L. (2014, January 24). 10 facts about Americans and public libraries. Retrieved August 29, 2016, from http://www.pewresearch.org/fact-tank/2014/01/24/10-facts-about-americans-and-public-libraries/

Rainie, L. (2015, September 22). Digital divides 2015. Retrieved August 29, 2016, from http://www.pewinternet.org/2015/09/22/digital-divides-2015/

Rothman, W. (n.d.). Wi-Fi versus your walls. Retrieved September 3, 2016, from https://www.thisoldhouse.com/ideas/wi-fi-versus-your-walls

Schwartz, M. (2013, May 10). Massive open opportunity: Supporting MOOCs in public and academic libraries. *Library Journal*. Retrieved September 3, 2016, from http://lj.libraryjournal.com/2013/05/library-services/massive-open-opportunity-supporting-moocs/#_

Seave, A. (2013, November 18). Are digital libraries a "winner-takes-all" market? OverDrive hopes so. *Forbes*. Retrieved August 29, 2016, from http://www

.forbes.com/sites/avaseave/2013/11/18/are-digital-libraries-a-winner-takes-all
-market-overdrive-hopes-so/#777d049f4a43

Smith, A. (2015, April 1). U.S. smartphone use in 2015. Retrieved August 29, 2016,
from http://www.pewinternet.org/2015/04/01/chapter-one-a-portrait-of-smart-
phone-ownership/

Sockel, A. (2014, January 22). Updated: Overdrive announces plan for audiobooks to
be solely available in mp3 format [blog]. Retrieved August 29, 2016, from http://
blogs.overdrive.com/front-page-library-news/2014/01/22/overdrive-announces
-plan-for-audiobooks-to-be-solely-available-in-mp3-format/

Solving the diversity dilemma: Changing the face of the STEM workforce. (2015,
February). *Vital Signs*. Retrieved August 29, 2016, from http://changetheequa
tion.org/sites/default/files/2015 Solving the Diversity Dilemma FINAL 6.2015
.pdf

Steele, K. (2014, September/October). The future of libraries and nontraditional
staffing models. *Young Adult Library Services, 11–15.*

Sullivan, M. (2013). *Library spaces for 21st-century learners: A planning guide for
creating new school library concepts*. Chicago: American Association of School
Libraries.

Tanzi, N. (2016). *Making the most of digital collections through training and outreach: The innovative librarian's guide.* Santa Barbara, CA: Libraries Unlimited.

TechSoup for Libraries. (n.d.-a). Technology assessments. Retrieved August 29, 2016,
from   http://www.techsoupforlibraries.org/cookbook-3/planning-and-decision
-making/technology-assessments

TechSoup for Libraries. (n.d.-b). Strategic and technology plans. Retrieved September 2, 2016, from http://www.techsoupforlibraries.org/cookbook-3/planning
-and-decision-making/strategic-and-technology-plans

Tor. (n.d.). Overview. Retrieved September 3, 2016, from https://www.torproject
.org/about/overview.html.en

Urban Libraries Council. (2012). Unified service and tiered information service. Retrieved September 2, 2016, from http://www.urbanlibraries.org/unified-service
-and-tiered-information-service-innovation-142.php?page_id=38

Urban Libraries Council. (2013). Cupertino Library's tech toolbar. Retrieved September 2, 2016, from http://www.urbanlibraries.org/cupertino-library-s-tech
-toolbar-innovation-854.php?page_id=175

U.S. Department of Justice. (2010, September 15). 2010 ADA standards for accessible design. Retrieved September 3, 2016, from https://www.ada.gov/regs2010/2
010ADAStandards/2010ADAStandards_prt.pdf

Valentino-Devries, J., Singer-Vine, J., & Soltani, A. (2012, December 24). Websites
vary prices, deals based on users' information. Retrieved September 3, 2016,
from https://msu.edu/~conlinmi/teaching/MBA814/WSJpricediscriminat

Watson-Lakamp, P. (2015). *Marketing moxie for librarians: Fresh ideas, proven techniques, and innovative approaches*. Santa Barbara, CA: Libraries Unlimited.

Weber, L. (2015). What do workers want from the boss? [blog]. *The Wall Street
Journal*. Retrieved September 2, 2016, from http://blogs.wsj.com/atwork/2015
/04/02/what-do-workers-want-from-the-boss/?mod=e2tw

West, J. C. (2011). *Without a net: Librarians bridging the digital divide*. Santa Barbara, CA: Libraries Unlimited.

Wilder, S. (2013, June 24). The end of lower skill employment in research libraries. *Library Journal*. Retrieved February 24, 2017, from http://lj.libraryjournal .com/2013/06/opinion/backtalk/the-end-of-lower-skill-employment-in -research-libraries-backtalk/#_

Williment, K. (2013, April 26). It takes a community to build a library. *Public Librar- ies Online*. Retrieved August 29, 2016, from http://publiclibrariesonline.org /2013/04/it-takes-a-community-to-build-a-library/

Zickuhr, K., Rainie, L., & Purcell, K. (2013, January 22). Library services in the digital age. Retrieved September 2, 2016, from http://libraries.pewinternet .org/2013/01/22/library-services/

Zickuhr, K., Rainie, L., Purcell, K., Madden, M., & Brenner, J. (2012, June 22). Li- braries, patrons, and e-books. Retrieved September 2, 2016, from http://libraries .pewinternet.org/2012/06/22/part-1-an-introduction-to-the-issues-surrounding -libraries-and-e-books/

Index

About the Author

NICK D. TAYLOR is the supervisor of tech experience at Arapahoe Libraries. In his travels as a technology advocate for public libraries, he has taught computer classes, helped create makerspaces, demonstrated beta technology, and learned from as well as been inspired by supervising a technology specialist team.